Praise for Get Up To Speed With Online Marketing

'Not to be part of the social media revolution is to miss out. Jon Reed really gets it and shows you how to join in.'

Suzanne Moore, Columnist, *Mail on Sunday*

'...ast-paced digital world where it seems like everyone is playing catch up, *Get Up To Speed With Online Marketing* is packed with the practical, no-nonsense insight that allows anyone marketing their business not only to keep up but to get ahead.'

Justin Cooke, CEO, Fortune Cookie and Chair, British Interactive Media Association

'Why waste money and resources trying to tweak your marketing strategy for the online age? Jon Reed has done it for you by giving you the tools to join the social marketing revolution taking place. This practical and invaluable book should be on the desk of anyone wanting to make a success of their online presence.'

Claudio Concha, Head of New Media, Big Lottery Fund

'Facebook, LinkedIn, Twitter or YouTube? If you want to figure out how to effectively use social media to build your business, Jon Reed's straightforward and practical guide will help you figure out which one to use and where to start.'

Suzanne Kavanagh, Skillset

Get up to speed with online marketing

How to use websites, blogs, social networking and much more

Jon Reed

**Financial Times
Prentice Hall
is an imprint of**

Harlow, England • London • New York • Boston • San Francisco • Toronto • Sydney • Singapore • Hong Kong
Tokyo • Seoul • Taipei • New Delhi • Cape Town • Madrid • Mexico City • Amsterdam • Munich • Paris • Milan

PEARSON EDUCATION LIMITED

Edinburgh Gate
Harlow CM20 2JE
Tel: +44 (0)1279 623623
Fax: +44 (0)1279 431059
Website: www.pearsoned.co.uk

First published in Great Britain in 2011

ISBN: 978-0-273-73264-8

British Library Cataloguing-in-Publication Data
A catalogue record for this book is available from the British Library

Library of Congress Cataloging-in-Publication Data
Reed, Jon, 1971-
  Get up to speed with online marketing : how to use websites, blogs, social networking and much more / Jon Reed.
    p. cm.
  Includes index.
  ISBN 978-0-273-73264-8 (pbk.)
  1. Internet marketing. 2. Social media. 3. Small business--Management. I. Title.
  HF5415.1265.R43 2011
  658.8'72--dc22
                    2010034354

10 9 8 7 6 5 4 3 2 1
14 13 12 11 10

Typeset in 9pt Stone serif by 30
Printed in Great Britain by Henry Ling Ltd, at the Dorset Press, Dorchester, Dorset

Contents

Acknowledgements

I would like to thank the business owners who generously shared their experiences of online marketing with me for this book, and continue to do so by contributing case studies to the website. I would also like to thank Liz Gooster, Martina O'Sullivan, Emma Devlin and Anna Campling at FT Prentice Hall for their support, and my friends and family for their patience while I was writing *Get Up To Speed With Online Marketing*. I'm also grateful to the many people who tweeted encouragement while I was writing, and everyone who has taken my workshops, attended my lectures, read my blogs and followed me on Twitter. It's a pleasure to be part of your social network. This book is for you.

Publishers's acknowledgements

We are grateful to the following for permission to reproduce copyright material:

Figures 6.1 and 15.13 from WordPress. WordPress is a registered trademark of the WordPress Foundation; Figure 11.1 from Facebook with the permission of Snapdragon. Facebook is a Trademark of Facebook Inc.; Figures 13.1, 13.6, 13.8, 13.9, 13.11 and 13.13 from Twitter with the permisison of the Tweeters; Figure 13.14 from TweetDeck; Figures 15.7, 15.8, 15.9, 15.10, 15.11 from Digg.

In some instances we have been unable to trace the owners of copyright material, and we would appreciate any information that would enable us to do so. Every effort has been made to trace the copyright holders and we apologise in advance for any unintentional omissions. We would be pleased to insert the appropriate acknowledgement in any subsequent edition of this publication.

About the author

Jon Reed is a social media consultant, trainer, lecturer, writer and blogger. He previously worked in publishing for 10 years, including as publishing director for McGraw-Hill. He runs the following businesses:

- **Reed Media** (www.reedmedia.eu) – a social media consultancy business, offering social media production and training.
- **Small Business Studio** (www.smallbusinessstudio.co.uk) – a web design, branding and marketing agency for start-ups and entrepreneurs.
- **Publishing Talk** (www.publishingtalk.eu) – a blog and online community of authors and publishers interested in social media, digital publishing and the future of the industry.

He also blogs about anything else that interests him at www.jonreed.co.uk, and can be found on most social networking sites. Follow him on Twitter at @jonreed or @getuptospeed and find links to him on the other social sites he uses at www.getuptospeed.biz.

Introduction

Traditional marketing doesn't work: get over it!

Forget everything you've heard about marketing. Put away those mar-keting plans, cancel that magazine ad, and stop buying mailing lists. Traditional marketing doesn't work. It's expensive and ineffective. In today's attention economy, people screen out magazine ads, they Sky+ or Tivo out TV ads, ignore billboards and throw away your carefully crafted direct mail campaign with the rest of the junk mail. They spend more and more time online – especially on social networking sites. While you're trying to attract new business, they're updating their Facebook profiles and 'tweeting' their every thought on Twitter.

If you're a small business owner, this is good news. You can go where your market is and save money by focusing your marketing efforts online. If you can make your products or services easy to find online, you're halfway there. This book will show you how to get started right now with the new online marketing tools.

This book has a focus on the new marketing: the new low-to-no cost online tools like blogs, podcasts, Facebook, YouTube and Twitter. These are not simply the latest online marketing tools, but a fundamentally new approach to marketing. But this is not a trend-chasing manifesto for seeking out the latest shiny new online toy. The focus is firmly on your marketing strategy, rather than on the tools for their own sake. Not every tool is right for every business. And although it covers the wide range of the new tools available, it puts them in the wider context of online marketing: building your website, using search engine marketing, and creating a winning email campaign are equally important. Many of your activities on Twitter, Facebook, YouTube, etc. will be aimed at driving traffic to your website, or encouraging people to sign up to your email newsletter. These things work best together.

The marketing revolution

What we are witnessing is nothing short of a marketing revolution. Instead of indiscriminately shouting sterile corporate marketing messages at people who may or may not be interested in your product or service, today you can find people who are *already interested* in what you have to offer, by tapping into online communities of interest. In today's competitive marketplace you need to be findable. You need to go where your customers are, and engage them in a two-way dialogue.

The first era of marketing was *mass marketing* – the dawn of advertising as we know it, where average products were repeatedly advertised to the largest possible number of average people, using mass communication methods, particularly television. Anyone who has seen the US TV series *Mad Men* will have some insight into those heady days of the first ad agencies.

The second phase was *direct marketing* – a far more focused approach of segmenting and targeting a particular market, creating marketing lists, and then bombarding them with junk mail (er, I mean direct mail). While more targeted, this is still an interruption of people's attention.

We are now in the era of *social marketing*. We can still reach targeted markets – even more niche than before, in fact – but the difference now is that we are not so much interrupting them, or even seeking permission to communicate with them, as creating communities around our products and services. We are making ourselves findable by these communities so that, instead of having to find, target and mail them, they come looking for us!

"we are now in the era of *social marketing* "

How did this come about? What is it about modern life that makes social marketing increasingly dominant? Humans are social creatures. We have a natural instinct to connect with others. Yet modern life is isolating. More than half of us live in cities. A third of us live alone. The days of gossiping with neighbours over the garden fence, or in the village store, seem to belong in a Miss Marple novel. More and more of us work from home or telecommute at least some of the time. Even if we have office colleagues, our multi-channel media milieu means we no longer have so many of those watercooler moments when we discuss last night's television with them. The trend is away from broadcasting towards narrowcasting – media that is individually tailored to our interests, needs and desires. Our every individual whim, taste and preference may be met – but where are the others who share our niche interests? Thanks to the Internet, we can now connect with them.

Because social media is a personal medium where authenticity matters, it is not always easy for big corporations to use – and some have got it really, really wrong. It's perfect if you're a small business or entrepreneur: you can build trust and make connections by using your personality, and being genuine.

Anyone with an Internet connection and a bit of creativity can now communicate with the world via the written word, audio, video and images. A radical power shift of content creation and distribution from large media institutions to individuals has taken place over the past few years: everyone is a publisher now. That's why *Time* magazine's Person of the Year in 2006 was YOU.

That content is the starting point for your online marketing campaign, as you use it to reach and engage with potential customers and clients who will seek it out with their online searches. The online marketing revolution has arrived – and you can be part of it.

About this book

If you're a new or aspiring business owner, the challenges and tasks you face can appear daunting. How do you find time to market your product or service as well as doing the work required to deliver it? This book will show you quick wins, easy and effective ways to reach out to your market today. If you work for a larger business, you will also find plenty of tips here to inform and inspire and you – and help you avoid common pitfalls.

You may already use sites and services like Facebook, YouTube, Twitter, Flickr and iTunes to keep in touch with friends, share photos or download music – but wonder how such sites can be used for marketing your business. The range of online marketing tools out there can seem bewildering. Where do you start? How do you cut through the hype?

This book shows you what works, why it works, and how to use it. It takes you step by step through the process of choosing and using online marketing tools effectively. For each tool covered, there are also tips on managing the workload (just where *will* you find the time for all those updates?) and measuring your results. An extensive glossary cuts through the jargon; and if you're not quite ready to take the plunge yourself, it also advises you on how to find someone to do it for you.

We will look at case studies of businesses that have succeeded with online marketing tools, in the '...in action' section of each chapter. The case studies and other businesses mentioned along the way in this book may surprise you: most are not technology businesses, as you might imagine. They include clothing retailers, farmers, food producers, a hypnotherapist, a photographic gallery, a wedding stationery supplier, a jigsaw retailer and a coffee shop owner – people just like you. And if you think that no one in your industry bothers with the new online marketing methods, that's brilliant news: you're in the privileged position of having a competitive advantage in your industry by being the first mover.

❝less marketing never leads to more sales❞
The new marketing isn't austerity marketing. But it does also have advantages when funds are tight. If your business is struggling as a result of the credit crunch or recession, it can be tempting to cut back on your marketing. Actually, it is the very worst time to do so. Less marketing never leads to more sales. However, by following the principles in this book, you will be able to cut back your marketing budget while increasing your reach.

The companion website – www.getuptospeed.biz

Online marketing is an ever-evolving field, with new social media tools cropping up all the time. It can be hard to keep up. For updates on all the information in this book, take a look at the accompanying website at www.getuptospeed.biz which includes:

- A blog with further advice on each of the online marketing tools covered in this book.
- Additional case studies from business owners.
- Video tutorials showing you how to use some of the online tools, such as WordPress and Twitter.

▦ A podcast featuring interviews with some of the business owners mentioned in this book.

▦ Essential planning tools and templates to help you think strategically about your marketing.

You can also get in touch with me via the site, and submit a case study sharing your own experience of online marketing. Some of these will make their way into the next edition.

Get in touch

Social media is a two-way conversation, and I want to hear from you! As the reader of this book, your opinion is the most important. Connect with me online, let me know what you did or didn't like, what you would like to see in the next edition, and tell me about your experience of online marketing.

You can also follow me on Twitter at @getuptospeed or @jonreed, find links to me on all the other social sites I use at www.getuptospeed.biz, or email me at jon@getuptospeed.biz.

For now, I wish you the best of luck with your business. Whether you're aspiring, brand new or more established, I hope you will find this book a useful guide for focusing your marketing efforts where they are most effective.

Get strategic

Online marketing 101

Before we jump in with all the exciting new tools available, let's take a step back and think about what you want to achieve. Too many people think: 'Everyone's blogging (or podcasting, tweeting, or on Facebook) – I should be blogging – let's start a blog!' This is the wrong starting point. Just because it's quick, easy, and free to set up an account with WordPress, Facebook, Twitter, MySpace or YouTube doesn't mean you should. Like any form of marketing, your starting point should be your marketing aims and objectives, then identifying your community and where they hang out, *then* you choose appropriate tools to reach them. This chapter will give you a crash course in online marketing strategy, and help you understand some key principles of social media that will enable you to use any tool appropriately and effectively.

What is online marketing?

There are almost two billion people online. Some of them are your ideal clients or customers. If you can reach even a tiny fraction of them, you will have a viable business. The Internet has brought enormous benefits to the way we market our businesses. A website is like a virtual shopfront that is always open. Email reaches targeted audiences with news of our latest products. A blog provides regularly updated information for customers and prospects, which they can comment on. People can listen to us wherever they are on an MP3 player. They can watch video demonstrations of our products online, now that massive take-up of broadband enables us to watch

> ** a website is like a virtual shopfront that is always open **

large streaming video files. Social networks enable us to make direct connections with people who are interested in our wares. We can reach niche audiences more easily than ever before – and the power of the Internet makes these niches global. However specialised our niche, there is a market for it online, which not only can we reach but, by increasing our visibility online, will also come looking for us.

Online marketing does a lot of the same things that traditional marketing does – it just does them more cheaply and effectively with a greater reach.

You may be familiar with the traditional marketing concept of the 'sales funnel'. It describes the stages through which you push potential customers from being a mass market of people who are unaware of your existence to a highly targeted loyal customer who comes back for more. It also describes which marketing methods to use at which stage.

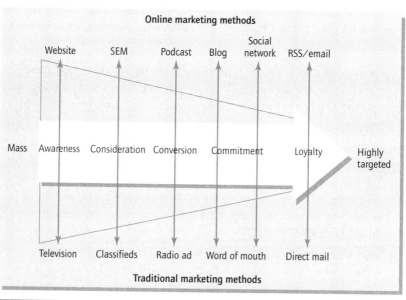

figure 1.1 Online vs. traditional marketing methods

Online marketing methods loosely map on to traditional methods, but at every stage you are making yourself visible to people who will seek you out, and engaging a highly targeted audience, rather than broadcasting an indiscriminate message and hoping for the best. Word of mouth is the Holy Grail of marketing – and very difficult to achieve offline. But it is turbo-charged with online marketing.

Why online marketing works for business

Online marketing is:

- **Affordable**. Because it is cheaper than traditional marketing, you can use it to punch above your weight.
- **Effective**. People spend more time online – use online marketing to reach your market where they are.
- **Authentic**. Tools such as social networks, blogging and podcasting are personal media. You can use them credibly as a small business owner, in a way that is hard for large corporates to do.

Given the amount of time people spend on the Internet, particularly on social sites such as Facebook and Twitter, it makes sense to join in. The average consumer tends to be way ahead of most businesses in their use of social media. If your market is spending time on these sites, so should you – go where your market is. Specific reasons why online marketing works for business include:

1 **Drive traffic to your site**. This is probably the single biggest reason for using online marketing. Your website is the hub of your business, and the aim of your online marketing activities is to drive traffic to it.

2 **New ways to connect with your market**. By establishing a presence on social sites that your market use, rather than taking an 'if you build it they will come' approach to your business website, you'll become visible to a new set of prospects.

3 **Build trust**. People always prefer to do business with people they know. Your clients and customers can get to know you through your online presence.

4 **Start a conversation**. Online marketing is a conversation – not a lecture. A two-way dialogue with your customers and prospects is much more effective than a one-way broadcast of your marketing message.

5 **Create value**. Part of the secret of online marketing is creating useful content and giving it away. If you can create a useful resource or interesting content targeted at your niche, they will keep coming back for more.

6 **Build communities and relationships**. Think of your market as a 'community of interest', built around a particular topic related to your business. You may also be able to create a community around your business or product – if it is interesting enough!

7 **Provide quick, up-to-date information about your business or topic of interest.** The 'breaking news' aspect of many forms of online marketing makes it ideal for announcements about new products or services, special offers, or simply valuable topical information about your sector or area of expertise.

8 **Data capture.** Building a database of potential customers is a core aim of your email marketing campaign. But much of your online marketing effort will also be geared towards list building – not just your lists of Facebook fans and Twitter followers, but the calls to action you will use to encourage people to sign up to your email newsletter.

9 **Market research.** One of the benefits of using the new online marketing tools is that is you are much closer to your market and aware of what they want. But you can go a stage further and ask them for their feedback on your products or services, or even create an online questionnaire and market it through your online marketing channels.

10 **Low-cost, low-risk, effective.** Most of the tools are available either free or very cheap. The investment is often in time rather than money. The risks of using a social media and communicating openly with your market are low, so long as you follow the principles in this book. They are far outweighed by the benefits you will gain. For anyone still concerned about maintaining control, it is important to remember that we have already lost control – and probably never really had it in the first place. People are already talking about us. It is important for you to be aware of where those conversations are taking place, to join them, and to influence them where appropriate.

Reaching niche markets online

Another benefit of online marketing is the ability to create a viable business out of a niche market. Niches work well online, and it's easier than ever before to reach them. You may have heard of Chris Anderson's concept of *The Long Tail*[1]. It's a variation of the 80/20 rule, applied to the revenue generated by a product range. Typically, 80 per cent of your revenue will come from 20 per cent of your products. A small number of 'bestsellers' generates more income than a large number of low-selling

---

1 Chris Anderson (2006) *The Long Tail: how endless choice is creating unlimited demand*, Random House Business Books.

items. A frequency distribution of number of products by volume of sales is not a new idea. What's new is the idea that the 'long tail' of low-sellers can now be profitable – and even make more money than the 'head' of blockbuster items – thanks to the low distribution costs of selling online. Amazon is a classic case of this, where a seemingly infinite variety of niche products reach a niche audience, and their low unit sales volumes over time combine to make these products not only viable but also a nice earner. If your business has an identifiable niche, and you can provide products or services at a distance, you too can benefit from the Long Tail by using online marketing to reach your community.

What is social media?

Although I've so far been talking about 'the new online marketing tools', these are more properly referred to as *social media*. Social media is simply a collection of free, online tools and platforms that people use to publish, converse and share content online. It's what we used to call 'Web 2.0' – a second generation of more collaborative online tools.

Social media tools include blogs, podcasts, online video, photo-sharing sites, social networks, virtual worlds and social bookmarking sites – all the tools covered in this book from Chapter 6 onwards.

You might also think of social media as a collection of websites and online services: Facebook, LinkedIn, MySpace, Twitter, Flickr, Second Life, iTunes, Delicious, StumbleUpon and so on. For our purposes, it is most helpful to think of it as an approach to marketing, and a subset of online marketing tools which, more broadly, include websites, search engine marketing and email marketing.

> **❝ people today think in a Googlesque way ❞**

It is a shift from 'push' marketing, where we are pushing a marketing message at people, to 'pull' marketing, where we are attracting people towards us with engaging, interesting, valuable content that people will seek out. People today think in a Googlesque way – they seek out what interests them. If you can tap into those communities of interest, you won't ever need to sell again – people will come looking for you.

You might think of it as permission-based marketing, word-of-mouth marketing, or conversational marketing. One phrase I came across a little while ago on the conference circuit is *martini marketing* – though it's one that I shall have to stop using in lectures and workshops, since most people I speak to these days are too young to get the reference! There was a TV advertising campaign for Martini in the 1970s which used the strap line: 'any time, anyplace, anywhere'. That really sums up how marketing should work these days – going where your market is, reaching them with content they want, when and where they want you to.

This is a shift away from *megaphone marketing* – randomly shouting your message at a heterogeneous mass of people who may or may not be interested in what you have to say. By using social media, you are making yourself visible to people who are already interested in what you have to say. You can tap into these communities of interest, engage them with useful content, and build a relationship with them.

Social media marketing works for small businesses because it focuses on building customer relationships rather than sterile marketing campaigns. Resist the temptation to use that safe, impersonal corporate voice – stick your head above the parapet and be yourself!

Social media myths

We've come a long way in a very short space of time with social media. The World Wide Web has only been around for about 20 years. And social media as we know it has only really been around since 2006 – the year that *Time* magazine nominated their Person of the Year as 'You'. The year 2006 was a significant one in social media: Facebook opened its network to anyone, rather than just US college kids; Twitter launched; and a new company called YouTube was bought by Google. These are now three of the biggest sites on the Internet. Yet some of the early myths about social media still persist. Let's dispel a couple of them now.

Myth #1 – It's just for kids

Business got very excited about social media a few years ago, when there was a lot of talk of the 'MySpace Generation' – i.e. using social media to reach a young demographic of kids connecting online and creating media in their bedrooms. This may have been true in 2006 when

Facebook was a student network, but it is much less so now. The fastest-growing demographic in all social networks is people over the age of 35. On Facebook, 35–54-year-olds are growing the fastest, and 25–34-year-olds are doubling every six months. The largest age group on Twitter is 35–49-year-olds. Residents of the virtual world Second Life have an average age of 33; and members of LinkedIn an average age of 41 – as you might expect for a more professional network.

There are, of course, still plenty of young people on social networks. This generation of 'digital natives' were born into a world of digital technology. In a few years they are going to be your customers, your clients, your staff. Many of them already are. But the grown-ups are catching up. They might be thought of as 'digital immigrants', at varying levels of fluency in the new digital language.

❝ the grown-ups are catching up ❞

Myth #2 – It's a fad

I think we're now past the point where social media can be dismissed as a fad. It has simply become the way we use the Internet: in a social, interactive way. What is sometimes referred to as the 'social web' is really just the Web. We no longer say 'motor car' – we just say 'car'. It's taken as read that our cars are motorised. So it is becoming with the Web – it is a given that we use the Internet to connect with our friends, express our opinions, publish our photos or watch a video.

There is also hard research evidence to back up this new, social way we use the Internet. Social media channels have grown rapidly over the past year. According to a Nielsen report[2] in 2009, in the UK, social sites account for one in every six minutes the average Internet user spends online. Facebook is the most popular social network globally, with 500m active users, and Twitter is the fastest-growing social media tool, with an estimated 75m users at the time of writing. You can find the latest user statistics on Facebook at http://www.facebook.com/press/info.php?statistics.

---

2 Nielsen, March 2009, http://www.nielsen-online.com/pr/pr_090309.pdf (PDF).

Core principles of social media

There are certain unwritten rules of using social media, and people don't like it when you break them. Understanding of the culture of social media is important. If you adhere to the following principles, you shouldn't go too far wrong, whichever tool you use:

1 **Be authentic, open, transparent.** If there's one thing you take away from this book, it is to be authentic at all times. Don't pass yourself off as something or someone you're not. Behave in a professional way, but don't be afraid to use your personal voice. The good thing about being a small business is that you don't need to get your communications approved by a committee or signed off by five people. You can just do it. Be yourself, be authentic, and people will trust you. We live in an age where trust is no longer in big institutions but in 'people like me'.

2 **Don't go for the hard sell.** Don't spam a Facebook group with your marketing message – provide useful content that your community will value.

3 **Build social currency.** The best way to get a feel for social media is simply to use it. What's more, establishing a social media presence gives you 'permission' to use it for marketing. Once you have been on various social sites for a while, you have more credibility: people will take you more seriously and listen to what you have to say.

4 **Don't view it as just another marketing channel.** Social media is a fundamentally different approach to marketing. Using it is a commitment – not a tactic or a campaign.

5 **Don't treat it as a one-way broadcast medium.** Yes, you can issue press releases using blogging software – but that's not really a blog. You can just use Twitter as an automatic feed from your blog – but that's not the most engaging way to use it. Social media becomes much more interesting, and effective, when it facilitates a two-way conversation between you and your community of interest.

6 **Be clear about responsibilities.** If you are a micro-business or sole trader, it will probably be you maintaining all of this. But if there are several of you working on the business, it pays to be clear about who is responsible for updating what, and how often.

7 **Be patient.** Social media needs a long-term approach. A new blog takes a good six months to establish itself and build a following. You will

need to spend time and effort building and maintaining your online presence before it translates into sales. But that online presence, once established, will continue to build and provide you with an essential source of potential clients and customers, highly targeted within your community of interest, who will come looking for you.

Never mind the tech

Finally, please don't worry about the technical side of things. Most of it is quite easy, and I'll take you step-by-step through the most important bits. You can also find more advice and tutorials on the website at www.getuptospeed.biz. And you can always find other people to help out, whether your in-house IT person, an external consultant or a 'virtual assistant' (see Chapter 16 for more advice on this).

It really is about your business, your passions, your ideas – rather than the technology. I am not a geek. I don't get excited by technology for its own sake. I am interested in using the most effective, easy, affordable marketing tools for my businesses. Most of them **you don't need to** happen to be online tools. You don't need to be a **be a tech head to use** tech head to use social media. It's more important **social media** to have a message, some compelling content and a bit of creativity. The rest you can learn as you go along. Most of the tools are quite easy to pick up. This is another area where the 80/20 rule applies: 80 per cent of social media is content; 20 per cent is technology.

The content that you reach people with is more important than the tools you use to reach them. Tapping into communities of interest is a key goal of social media marketing. And communities are built around content, not technology.

Your online marketing plan

Y ou know that dreadful management-speak mantra: 'Fail to plan and plan to fail'? Well, there is some truth in it. If you don't spend a bit of time planning your online marketing, you may not fail, but you will probably waste valuable time that you could have spent doing something more useful. You risk ploughing through loads of very interesting information on, say, Twitter, only to discover that Twitter isn't really a useful tool for your business.

Don't worry – it won't take long, and you can get started with a simple one-page online marketing plan. You can find a template for this on the companion website.

Until quite recently, it was common practice to simply jump in and start using the next, new social media tool, whether it was podcasting, Twitter, or Second Life. But there is also now an emerging body of best practice and, by following it, you can save wasted time and effort and avoid embarrassment. There are some real howlers out there – examples of businesses who have not looked before they leaped, and got it very wrong. I applaud their enthusiasm – at least they're having a go. But it can backfire horribly. Many have learned from their experience, and gone on to create successful social media campaigns. You can learn from their mistakes. Being open to risk and unafraid of criticism is part of what this journey is about: make mistakes, learn quickly, move on.

It is understandable why business owners often ask themselves, say, 'How can we use Facebook?' rather than 'How can we reach our market?' Every new technology brings with it a search for ways to use it. But this is not the most effective starting point.

Five questions to ask yourself before you start

Your approach, and the questions you ask yourself, should be just the same as for any of your marketing efforts:

1 **What are my marketing aims and objectives?** Like any form of marketing, this is the starting point – not the marketing tool itself.

2 **Who is my target market?** Know your audience. What is your niche? What unique value can you offer?

3 **Where can I find them?** Where does your market hang out? Use online tools to find your community of interest and tap into it.

4 **Which tools are most appropriate to use?** Which tools will both reach your market and be possible for you to manage realistically?

5 **How will I measure my results?** How will you know if you are successful? What metrics will you use?

Note that the choice of tool comes way down the list. It pays to think strategically about how you choose and use tools described in this book.

The other reason for not simply jumping in and blogging, tweeting or networking is that there is an art and etiquette to these things. It is important to understand the *culture* of social media – it is all too easy to misjudge when, where and how to use social media, and end up annoying people by spamming them on Twitter with your marketing message rather than engaging your community of interest with useful content. Stick to the core principles of social media and you won't go far wrong.

❝ it is important to understand the *culture* of social media ❞

Choosing your tools

Now you need to choose your weapons. But with so many tools out there, and new versions and variants springing up all the time, where do you start? How do you find out what works for you? It is important to go where your market is. But not everyone has time to maintain a blog. Not everyone is an aspiring DJ and feels comfortable podcasting. What can you do to reach out to your market online authentically, effectively and efficiently?

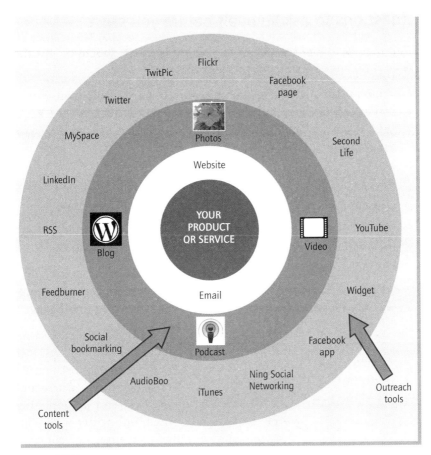

figure 2.1 Choosing online marketing tools

At the centre of things is your product or service – the thing you want to sell. Wrapped around that is your business website – the centrepiece of your online marketing. The ultimate aim of most of your marketing effort is to drive people here. One of the things you will use to do this is search engine marketing (SEM), using tools such as Google AdWords.

Another key aim is to build an email marketing list. Your email newsletter will provide specific calls to action leading people to buy from you – and most often will also drive people to your site. And the main call to action on your website will be to sign up to your newsletter.

The next three chapters of this book look at how to get online with a website (Chapter 3), boost your search engine results with SEM (Chapter 4), and create an engaging email marketing campaign (Chapter 5).

Everything else is social media, which the rest of the book focuses on. Your social media efforts will be geared to driving people to your website, and to encouraging them to sign up to your email newsletter. These will be the most common calls to action you will use. But the proliferation of social media marketing tools now available is bewildering – and ever growing. Where do you start? Which will you use? It helps simplify things if you categorise them into *content tools* and *outreach tools*.

- **Content tools** comprise the four main content types found on the Internet: text, images, audio and video – which in social media translate into the content you will create: blogs, photo sharing (e.g. on Flickr), podcasts and online video (e.g. on YouTube). It is important to provide useful, informative, valuable content that is findable and 'pass-on-able' by the communities of interest you want to reach. We will look at content tools in Part three: Get creative (Chapters 6–9).

- **Outreach tools** are, essentially, everything else – but particularly social networks such as Facebook, LinkedIn and Twitter. Virtual worlds such as Second Life may also work for some businesses, and encouraging people to pass on your content with social bookmarking buttons ('share on Facebook', 'Tweet this', 'Digg this', etc.) gets the word out. You will use these tools to disseminate and raise awareness of the social media content you create, as well as engaging your community in conversation. We will look at outreach tools in Part four: Get out there (Chapters 10–15).

Find out what your market is using by doing some keyword searches on social sites. Discover what works for you, what you feel comfortable with, and have the time and inclination to use. Then make sure you use at least one content tool, and at least one outreach tool.

You can go a stage further and also categorise social media tools into *listening tools* and *measurement tools:*

- **Listening tools** are what you use to gain market intelligence, 'listen in' on conversations that are taking place about you or your business sector, and find existing online communities. For big brands, such as Coca-Cola or Nike, listening tools may be the main thrust of their social media marketing – listening to what people are saying about them, joining and influencing those conversations, and responding appropriately. These tools may be the standard outreach tools such as Twitter, Facebook and Delicious, which you can do searches on; plus services such as www.technorati.com or Google Blog Search (http://blogsearch.google.com) to find blogs. You can keep up with relevant blogs in your area by subscribing to their RSS feeds; and use Google Alerts (www.google.com/alerts) to monitor whatever interests you online by keyword. Use www.socialmention.com to monitor keywords across a range of social media in real time, and to sign up to 'social media alerts' – like Google alerts but for social media.

■ **Measurement tools** are any online tool you use to measure the results of your marketing. These may include some of the metrics built in to Facebook or YouTube, web services such as www.twittercounter.com, www.tweetstats.com or www.twitteranalyzer.com to analyse your Twitter statistics, or your web-stats package such as Google Analytics (www.google.com/analytics) or Clicky Web Analytics (www.getclicky.com).

Effective online marketing

It's not just the tools you use, but how you use them. To make your online marketing work hard for you, do the following:

1 **Engage people with valuable content.** Create content that people will value and pass on. This may be in the form of blogs, photos, podcasts or video. There is a bit of a myth about viral marketing – it doesn't have to be videos of people dancing on running machines, baby pandas sneezing, or other cool stuff the kids will pass on. It just has to be useful to someone. Interesting, engaging and informative, and likely to help your target market in some way. That may be a blog post explaining how recent tax changes affect businesses. It may be a video demonstration. It may simply be a link to a useful news article shared on Twitter.

2 **Be findable.** Search isn't just about Google – people also search on YouTube, Twitter, Facebook, iTunes and elsewhere. Having a presence on these sites improves your chances of being found. But also make sure your social media channels are easy to find – link between them, and include a little 'social media cloud' of icons on your website that link to your presence on social sites. Then make it easy for other people to increase your findability: encourage pass-on by using social bookmarking buttons on blog posts (see Chapter 15).

3 **Use calls to action.** These are not used often enough in online marketing. You've gone to a lot of effort to get people on to your website – now tell them what you want them to do. That may be to sign up to your email newsletter, download something, buy something. Use calls to action on your social media too, at the end of blog posts, podcasts or video, or in your social networking status updates.

4 **Use multiple tools** – their combined effect is greater than the sum of its parts.

Manage the workload

'This is all very well', you may say, 'but where on Earth am I going to find the time for all these blog posts and status updates?' It's a fair question. In our always-on culture, with a constant demand for information – and free information, at that – it can seem impossible to keep up. We will look at ways to manage the workload for each tool, but if you follow these general principles, you will be able to avoid working all hours like a social media Stakhanovite:

1 **Plan your media and resourcing.** Audit your existing social media, and reuse and repurpose material where possible.

2 **Encourage user-generated content,** whether Flickr photos, video responses on YouTube or blog comments.

3 **Share the workload** with multi-author blogs, and multiple logins and admins for Facebook pages or Twitter accounts.

4 **Leave a digital footprint wherever you go** – rather than updating multiple sites all the time. Use sites such as FriendFeed that aggregate your updates, RSS feeds and bookmarks – then import that feed to your Facebook page, or display it as an RSS widget on your blog.

5 **Use multiplier effects.** Automatically tweet your blog using www.twitterfeed.com. Pull your blog into Facebook using the Notes function or an RSS app. Make your Twitter status automatically become your Facebook status.

6 **Integrate social media into your working life** with desktop applications such as www.tweetdeck.com.

7 **Set aside time.** Finally, there is no substitute for finding time. Set aside time to work on your social media as you would for any other marketing activity.

Finally, don't be afraid to ask for help if you need it. There are online tools to help you do that too, which we will look at in Chapter 16.

Measure success

How will you know when you have been successful? Social media metrics is a new and emerging field. The way you measure your results isn't always as obvious as counting the number of flyers returned. But there is plenty you can do to find out what works – and do more of it:

1 **Web analytics**. There's a lot you can tell from your standard webstats package such as Google Analytics. Not just about the number of visitors to your website, but the sources of that traffic. I use Clicky Web Analytics (www.getclicky.com), which I find useful for tracking social media sources.

2 **Bean counting**. How many Facebook fans, Twitter followers and LinkedIn connections do you have? How many people have viewed your YouTube video? How many downloaded your podcast? How many people have subscribed to your blog's RSS feed? These are fairly bald numbers, but will give you an idea of your reach.

3 **Rankings**. Where does your blog rank on www.technorati.com? Where does your Twitter account sit in relation to those other people in your industry on www.wefollow.com?

4 **Calls to action**. How many people actually answered that call to action? If you only made it in one place, on one channel, you know what proportion of readers/followers/members did as you asked.

5 **Surveys**. A more traditional method, but you can do some market research on the impact and awareness of your campaigns.

6 **Conversational index**. This applies to blogs, and is a measure of the level of engagement with your content. It is the number of comments divided by the number of blog posts – and you're aiming for a figure above 1. You can apply this to your whole blog, to a category, or a time period.

7 **Unique landing pages**. This is my favourite, and where things get really forensic. OK, so 1,000 people watched your YouTube video. You had a web address on the video notes on the YouTube page – but how many took action? If you include a web address at the end of the video, and make it a unique URL – i.e. a specific web address that is

only ever mentioned on that piece of video – but which automatically refers on to where you *actually* want people to land – you can see from your web stats exactly how many people not only watched the video, but also took action. You can use this method anywhere where you use a web address.

Your one-page marketing plan

You can write a 50-page marketing plan if you want. You can include a SWOT analysis, MoSCoW analysis, Boston Matrix and any other number of strategic theoretical tools that are beyond the scope of this book. Or you can actually do some marketing. Don't get me wrong – planning is a good thing, and if you're writing a college assignment or seeking investment you probably will need a longer document. But if, like most of us, you don't have the luxury of time, you can write your marketing plan in a single page. What's more, you should be able to distil your entire marketing plan into one page. It's a good discipline that will keep you focused on the core aims of your business.

> ❝ you can write your marketing plan in a single page ❞

Here are the things you need to focus on:

1 **Marketing aims and objectives.** What are you trying to do? Raise awareness of a new business? Differentiate yourself from the competition? Communicate the benefits of a new service?

2 **Positioning.** Where do you sit in relation to the competition?

3 **Target market.** Who is your ideal customer?

4 **Market niche.** Who is your community of interest? Where do they hang out?

5 **Marketing tools.** Which tools will you use to reach them?

6 **Calls to action.** What do you want them to do?

7 **Measuring success.** How will you know if you've been a success? What tools will you use to measure your results?

Here is your fill-in-the-blanks marketing plan template, which you can also download from the companion website, along with a sample filled-in form at www.getuptospeed.biz/plan.

The purpose of the marketing programme for _____ is to:

Our target market is:

Our community can be found at:

We plan to use the following social media marketing tools:

Tool *Pick at least one content tool (e.g. blog) and at least one outreach tool (e.g. Twitter)*	Call to action *E.g. sign up to newsletter; visit website*	Measurement *E.g. number of subscribers, group members, Twitter followers*
1.		
2.		
3.		
4.		
5.		

The rest of this book will look at the most important online marketing tools at your disposal.

Get online with:

- **Websites** – the point of most online marketing is to get people onto your website (Chapter 3).
- **Search engine marketing** – optimising your website to appear higher in search engine results, plus pay per click advertising such as Google AdWords (Chapter 4).
- **Email marketing** – the most important 'call to action' on your website is a newsletter sign-up form (Chapter 5).

Get creative and produce valuable content for your community with:

■ **Blogs** – business blogs generate traffic, build trust and position you as an expert (Chapter 6).

■ **Podcasts** – audio or video files that people subscribe to. Great for building a loyal following (Chapter 7).

■ **Online video** – connect with people on YouTube using video demonstrations, tutorials or testimonials (Chapter 8).

■ **Photo sharing** – use sites such as Flickr to showcase your products and encourage user-generated content (Chapter 9).

Get out there and spread the word with:

■ **Social networks** – choose and use sites such as Facebook, MySpace, LinkedIn and Twitter to build a community around your business and help people discover your products or services (Chapter 10).

■ **Facebook** – engage your community with pages, groups and events (Chapter 11).

■ **LinkedIn** – build professional contacts and sell business-to-business (Chapter 12).

■ **Twitter** – harness the power of the real-time web, and the fastest-growing social media tool (Chapter 13).

■ **Virtual worlds** – places like Second Life look like video games, but the 'characters' are avatars of real people behind their keyboards – people who you can sell to (Chapter 14).

■ **Social bookmarking** – sites such as Delicious, StumbleUpon or Digg where people can bookmark and share content they like. Include bookmarking buttons at the end of your blog postings to encourage pass-on (Chapter 15).

We will also look at sites and services that help you find someone to help you with all this in Chapter 16, and cut through the jargon with an A–Z of social media at the end of this book. Are you ready to get connected? Let's start with the foundation of all your online marketing: your website.

Take action

- **Define** your marketing goals.

- **Write** your one-page marketing plan.

- **Find** your community with **listening tools**.

- **Engage** your audience with **content tools**.

- **Distribute** your content with **outreach tools**.

- **Measure** your results with **measurement tools**.

- **Read on** to discover more about these tools, and choose the right ones for you!

part TWO

Get online

Establish a web presence
How to build a website with no technical knowledge

A website is the most important marketing tool for your business – if you do nothing else from this book, you absolutely must have a website. Fortunately it is much easier to establish a web presence than it used to be. There's no need to put this off for a lack of geeky coding experience: whether you hire a web developer or build it yourself using an easy-to-use content management system, creating and maintaining websites is more straightforward than ever. You can even add sophisticated functions such as shopping carts and event booking systems using low-cost third-party tools rather than having these coded into your website. And once you have your website, don't forget to spread the word with social media to draw people on to it. The web is about connecting people, and your website is about connecting them to your business.

❝ creating and maintaining websites is more straightforward than ever ❞

What is a website?

It is no longer sufficient to have a website to say you have an online presence – you also need to be present where your customers spend their time online, such as Facebook and Twitter. But a website is your essential starting point. The aim of all your other online marketing activities is to drive people to it, but it must also point outward to your presence elsewhere on the Internet. It is the hub of your online marketing activities. The other point of your website is to sell your products or services. Once you've gone to the trouble of getting people on to your website, you want to sell them something! Make your website your online point of sale.

Your market, your business and its needs will determine what sort of website you go for. Some options are:

A **brochure website** Websites used to be static collections of pages that happened to be published online, but might just as well have been printed. Today we expect more from a website than uploaded business stationery. We expect dynamic, ever-changing content. We also like to be involved in a two-way conversation rather than the passive recipient of a one-way broadcast. A brochure site will establish a web presence for you – but it's not going to get you as many leads as a dynamic website.

A **blog** This is like an online diary, with posts in reverse chronological order. But it is really just a special kind of website that you can update yourself – not just posts but pages. This means you can use blogging software such as WordPress as a content management system (CMS) to build an entire website. Whether your main business website is a blog or a traditional brochure website, the principles in this chapter apply to the content and approach of your site. We will look in more detail at blogging in Chapter 6.

An **e-commerce site** This is a website that is set up to sell products and take payments online. It is no longer necessary to invest a small fortune in creating a bespoke e-commerce site with your own shopping cart function coded from scratch. There is e-commerce software you can use on your site, or third-party websites you can use to sell through. It is now acceptable for any business to use PayPal to take payments on their websites without looking 'unprofessional'. You can even sell your products through an Ebay or Amazon store that you link to from your website. We will look at third-party websites and applications that you can use to extend your functionality later in this chapter.

Why a website is essential for business

A website is the most important marketing tool for your business. An online presence is a minimum requirement if you want to present a professional image, reach new customers and increase profits. A website:

■ is a 'shop window' that works for you 24 hours a day

■ enables you to reach a global market

■ promotes your products and services

▨ gives you credibility

▨ offers online support to your customers (which can save you time)

▨ provides a way for people to contact you.

Your clients and customers expect you to be online. How many times have people asked you for your web address, or said that they'll Google you? If you're not online, you don't exist. And they'll go to your competition, who are online.

---

websites in action

Studio 8 (www.studio8shop.com)

Studio 8 is an independent men's and women's fashion retailer in Primrose Hill, London. Their first website was a single brochure site: 'Just like a business card', says managing director Simon Savage who, in October 2009, decided 'Right – we have got to make something happen here', and invested in an e-commerce site.

Rather than create this from scratch, the new Studio 8 site was built with a third-party web service called Powa Instant Salesware (www.powa.com), which enables small business owners to create their own branded professional online store without any technical knowledge. 'Powa have templates that you can design yourself', says Simon, 'but I didn't want to feel I was just knocking up any old thing. I wanted something that looked professional.' He hired a designer recommended by Powa – Inspired Business Marketing (www.inspiredbusinessmarketing.com) – to create a unique design to reflect his company identity.

The same developer also custom designed a WordPress blog for Studio 8 (www.studio8darkside.com) to run alongside their Powa e-commerce site. Simon says: 'The blog allowed us to show our human side. We can share a little more about ourselves and our knowledge of fashion.'

The new e-commerce site went live in March 2010, and quickly paid for itself. Their web analytics show impressive results. Simon say: 'Before we went live with the Powa site, we had about 4,000 hits on our website in three years. Our Google analytics show that we have had more than this number in just three months, with around 40,000 pages viewed on the e-commerce site and over 1,000 hits on my blog. There's been an increased volume of email enquries, and every question I answer has the potential to turn into a sale. The e-commerce site meets all our criteria – ease of use, plenty of information, and good search engine recognition.'

> ▶ There are busy times when new season's stock comes in. But Powa's easy-to-use interface means that each item takes less than five minutes to describe, catalogue and enrich with search keywords. 'We're proud that our website holds its own against the bigger, more expensive sites that we admire. For the relatively small amount we invested, we've got the very best out of it', says Simon. 'I've learned that a website isn't just something you upload, leave and forget. It is about consolidating; you have to embrace it and nurture it just like a real bricks-and-mortar store.'
>
> **Get the idea**: Use third-party software and services such as WordPress for websites and blogs and Powa for e-commerce sites, rather than code from scratch. If you need something more tailored to your brand than the design templates offered, hire a designer to create a bespoke theme or template. This will still be far cheaper than hiring a developer to re-invent the wheel and code a new e-commerce site from the ground up. Include a blog on your e-commerce site to make a personal connection with your customers – people like to buy from people they feel they know.

Get up to speed with your website

So, how do you build a website with no technical knowledge? The short answer is you either hire a web designer, or build it yourself using a content management system such as WordPress. But doing it yourself isn't

❝ doing it yourself isn't for everyone ❞

for everyone, or suitable for every website. And there are other steps to think through. Do you have your own unique web address (domain name)? What content are you going to put on your website?

How will you structure it? What functions can you add using third-party tools? These are the steps you need to take:

1 Choose a domain name.

2 Hire a designer or do it yourself?

3 Write a design brief and plan your content.

4 Extend your functionality with third-party tools.

5 Get social: build connections and community.

Choose a domain name

It looks far more professional to have a proper email address on your business cards, such as joe@xyzwidgets.com rather than xyzwidgets@hotmail.com or xyzwidgets@gmail.com. For this, you need a domain name, which you can use for your website too. It is fine to start off just using it for email, before your website is ready (though people might come looking for it), but you must secure the domain name you want as soon as you can, before someone else takes it.

There are very many companies out there selling domain names and web hosting. www.godaddy.com, www.heartinternet.co.uk and www.123-reg.co.uk are popular, but do a search for one that suits you. Domain names and hosting are relatively cheap. Unless you're using a hosted service, such as http://wordpress.com, you will also need some web space to host your site at. The simplest way is to use the same company for both your hosting and domain name registration.

Hire a designer or do it yourself?

Unless web design is your specialism, it's rarely worth having a go yourself, and not worth your time to learn how to code websites. The exception to this is if you set up your website using a content management system such as WordPress, which can be a good way to set up a professional-looking web presence quickly.

If your website requires a lot of complex functionality, don't try this at home: hire a designer. There is advice on how to find someone in Chapter 16. The caveat here is that there is a range of third-party tools that can do many of these things for you, which we will look at later in this chapter.

quick win

Create your business site in minutes using WordPress

The quickest way to get a professional-looking website if you don't already have one is to put down this book right now and sign up for an account at http://wordpress.com.

Don't want to commit to a regular online diary? You can also use blogging software such as WordPress as a content management system to create 'traditional' websites, since you can add and update pages as well as blog posts. Want to update some of your web content? No need to call your web developer – just do it yourself with an easy-to-use interface. Write some text, add some links, upload some images, click 'Publish' and you're done. It really is that easy.

Using free tools such as WordPress, it is actually easier to build a dynamic business blogsite than the most basic static brochure site coded from scratch. There are, in fact, two versions of WordPress: http://wordpress.com, which is hosted on their servers and requires no technical knowledge; and http://wordpress.org, which you download for free and upload to your own server. We will look more at the pros and cons of each in Chapter 6.

Your design brief

The starting point for your website is your design brief. You should think this through and put some ideas down on paper before contacting a designer. The questions below are what a designer will ask. And even if you're doing it yourself, it's still a good discipline to go through this process. It will help you stay focused on the core aims and marketing objectives of your site. Think of it as a mini business plan for your website. Things to consider include:

> **❝ the starting point for your website is your design brief ❞**

1 What type of website do you want? E.g. a simple online brochure, an e-commerce site, a business blog?

2 What is the main purpose of your website? What are its marketing aims and objectives? E.g. establish a web presence, enhance your brand, position you as an expert, drive traffic, generate leads, capture data to build a marketing database? It will probably be a combination of all of the above!

3 What look and feel are you after? Should it follow a specific brand image or colour scheme? Which sites do you like the look and feel of? Spend some time looking at good and bad sites, and thinking about what you want for yours. While someone else's code and content is copyrighted, there's no reason you can't pick a site you like and copy the structure.

4 Who is your competition? What are their sites like? Who is your target audience? E.g. specific business sectors, individuals, current clients, prospective clients? Are you a business-to-business (B2B) or business-to-consumer (B2C) business?

5 What is your main 'call to action'? What do you want people to do once they arrive at your website? Buy something? Download a brochure? Watch a video demonstration? Sign up to a newsletter?

6 How many pages will your website have? E.g. home, about, contact, services, products, individual product pages, clients, news, etc. How will the site be structured?

7 What functionality do you need – e.g. a 'contact us' form, shopping cart functions, online booking system?

8 Do you already have images or do you need your designer to source these?

9 What media do you require? E.g. audio, video, Flash animation?

10 What is your schedule? Do you have a critical launch date, e.g. to coincide with a product launch or marketing campaign?

Plan your content

Even if you are putting pages together on a content management system, it pays to spend a bit of time first planning what content you want, and how you want it structured. What will your main pages be? What sub-pages? What content will appear on each?

Information architecture

A useful starting point is an information architecture (IA) diagram – a simple flowchart showing what goes where. You can do this as a simple sketch on a piece of paper. Here, for example, is a simple IA diagram for an imaginary image consultancy business:

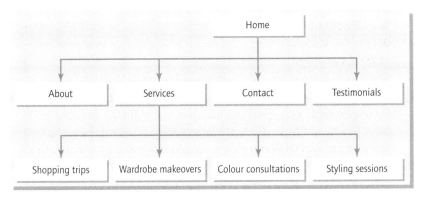

figure 3.1 Information architecture

It's a good idea to keep your Information Architecture shallow – i.e. don't give people too many layers to click through to get to key information. It should be easy and intuitive for people to get to your content quickly and easily. For a complex site, you might want to run your IA past a few people in your target market to make sure it makes sense.

Content

Key pages to consider for your website include:

Home page This should provide information about what you can offer your customers or clients, plus a brief overview of what else they can find on your site. This should also be obvious from your main navigation (the links to other pages on the site). Think also about your main call to action; make any special offers prominent on the home page and, if it is a selling site, make it easy to get to your product catalogue.

About us Tell your customers a bit about yourself, your business and its history, and your vision. If your business is closely linked to you personally, be sure to include a brief biography and headshot, plus links to your personal presence elsewhere on the Internet, such as your personal blog, Twitter account or Facebook profile.

Contact us Make it easy for people to reach you. Provide contact information in the footer of each page, with more detail on a dedicated Contact page. Include your mailing address, phone number and email address as a minimum. You may also want to include a contact form.

Products/Services A summary page of what you can offer, plus links to pages for individual products or services. Think about a call to action for each of these pages – such as a prominent 'buy now' button. See also **Shop** below.

Pricing This depends on what business you're in. If you're selling physical products, include clear pricing, and ideally a currency converter if you're selling internationally. It is not always so easy to price services online, but you could consider listing a range or minimum price if appropriate, such as '£50 +VAT per hour', 'from €650' or 'between $1,500 and $2,000'.

Search Include a search box prominently on your site, usually towards the top-right of the screen, so that visitors can look for the things they're interested in. This is particularly important if you have a lot of content on your site. If you're using WordPress, this function will be included. You can also add a Google custom search box to your site by going to www.google.com/cse and cutting and pasting the code.

Shop This might be a significant part of your site if your business sells products online, or a single page if you have just a few products you sell. Use PayPal 'buy now' buttons if you don't have many products, and consider more ambitious e-commerce options if you have a large store.

Testimonials/Reviews Include testimonials from current customers to show that you have a proven track record of delivering real benefits rather than theoretical ones. It helps reassure potential new clients. If you don't have any testimonials yet, email your clients and ask for feedback. You can also use LinkedIn to solicit recommendations (see Chapter 12), or create a short customer feedback form using www.surveymonkey.com. If you sell physical products, include product reviews.

Frequently asked questions (FAQs) These can help your customers learn more about what you do, your products and services, and help you spend less time answering queries by phone or email. If you have a complicated product, consider including online video demonstrations or tutorials somewhere on your site.

Press room If you regularly deal with the media (this might just be your local paper or radio station), send out press releases, or get requests for interviews or speaking, include a virtual press room on your website. This should include your press releases, a high-resolution headshot and 100 word biography of you and any other colleagues who might appear in the media, a paragraph of blurb about your business, and examples of any media appearances. Include a list of topics you speak on or would be happy to be interviewed about.

Event calendar If you regularly run events, such as seminars, product launches or demonstrations, or exhibitions, include an event calendar so that customers know when you are coming to a town near them. A calendar is also useful if you make regular client visits. Saville Row tailor Thomas Mahon uses one on his www.englishcut.com website to publicise his US trips. Likewise, tailors King and Allen list their 'fitting days' all over the UK at www.kingandallen.co.uk.

Blog Your website may include a blog as a subsection (e.g. www.mybusiness .com/blog) or link to a blog on a separate domain name, or your entire site may be a blog, with the latest posts appearing on the front page. If your blog is separate from your main site, you can still pull in extracts of your latest couple of blog posts on to your home page to highlight your blog and to keep your content fresh. We will look at blogging in more detail in Chapter 6.

Newsletter There are a couple of options here:

- A **Latest news** section on your site can be driven by blogging software even if you don't want a blog per se. You can also deliver the latest news posts automatically by email using a service called www.feedburner.com.

- An **email newsletter** goes one stage further, and if you make it exclusive to subscribers you can include special offers and discounts that only apply to newsletter recipients. We will look more at email newsletters in Chapter 5.

Resources Share some useful content in your field of expertise, such as market reports, white papers or other documents than can be downloaded for free, or in exchange for signing up to your email newsletter. Use these as an opportunity to position yourself as an expert and share useful information without too much of a hard sell. Depending on your business, it may even be possible to sell some of these – though make sure you always keep at least some of your content free.

Widgets A widget is a discrete bit of code from another website that adds a specific function to yours. Commonly used on blogs, they can be used on any website too. Widgets include Facebook badges, latest blog postings or tweets, photos from your Flickr account, relevant products from Amazon linked to your Amazon affiliate account, and so on. Very easy to use, just copy and paste the code supplied into your website to add extra functionality without having to invent it yourself.

Site map For a large site with many subpages, a site map can help people find the information they need. It should be set out as a list of text links, with subpages indented.

Legal boilerplate In addition to any statutory declarations required of your company name, address and registration number, it is good practice to include a privacy policy and an accessibility statement. See www.getup tospeed.biz/policies for examples.

Extend your website's functionality with third-party tools

Why reinvent the wheel? Do you really need you own, bespoke, lovingly hand-coded web form, shopping cart or event booking system? There was a time when you had to do it all yourself because (a) it looked more professional; and (b) things like PayPal didn't exist.

Today, even large organisations use third-party web services to fulfil key, specialised functions of their businesses online. They do it better and cheaper than you could yourself. And nobody

❝ they do it better and cheaper than you could yourself ❞ minds any more – these sites are trusted, and can actually make you look more professional than if you attempt it yourself. What's more, many can be branded to your business. Most are very easy to use, and will provide you with full, easy-to-follow instructions. Most will also provide you with a bit of code that you just need to copy and paste into your website or CMS.

Here are my top five third-party websites and services to consider for your business:

1. PayPal (www.paypal.com) What did we do before PayPal? There is no longer any need to develop complex credit card merchant scripts on your website to sell things online. In fact, it is better not to, since PayPal is a more trusted and more secure way of taking payments online. With a PayPal business account, you have access to a range of merchant services, from simple 'buy now' buttons to more complex shopping cart functions. You can also send customers invoices using your PayPal account. They don't even have to have a PayPal account in order to pay you – just a credit card. Other online payment solutions include Google Checkout, ClickBank and WorldPay.

PayPal is simple and affordable to use, and has lots of features, including '3 click' payments, the ability to issue refunds, track parcels and print postage labels. Its shopping cart feature, however, is fairly basic, and doesn't offer options such as discount codes and vouchers. If you want more sophisticated features, consider installing some shopping cart software that integrates with PayPal.

2. E-Junkie (www.e-junkie.com) E-junkie is a web-based service that provides shopping cart and buy now buttons, and is suitable for both physical products and digital downloads. Use it to sell on your own website, or even on eBay or MySpace. For digital downloads such as ebooks, mp3 files and software, it will sort out the delivery of files and codes for you; for physical products it will calculate shipping and manage inventory. **Powa** (www.powa.com) is another web-based service that enables you to create a branded, professional online store without technical knowledge – but will also help you find a designer if you need something more bespoke. Other e-commerce solutions are based on installing software on your own site, including **Actinic**, **ZenCart**, **osCommerce** and **CubeCart**. But if you don't want to bother with uploading and configuring software, use a web-based solution for e-commerce.

3. Wufoo (http://wufoo.com) If you need a form or questionnaire embedding in your website, particularly if you want to collect payments at the same time with PayPal, use Wufoo. Useful if you want clients to brief you on a project online – and pay you in advance at the same time – or for taking orders or event registrations. It is used by some big clients such as Disney, Sony and The Washington Post.

4. Eventbrite (www.eventbrite.com) Many organisations who once sold tickets on their own website are now using Eventbrite. It is even used by CNN, FedEx and NASA. It is probably the best-known web service for promoting events and selling them online. I use it all the time for my workshops. Add details of your event, set the pricing, and you're good to go. Customers can pay online, by linking to your PayPal account – or they can request a traditional invoice.

5. Google Maps (http://maps.google.com / http://maps.google.co.uk) If you want to include a map of your business on your Contact Us page, why not make it an interactive Google map? Mine is at www.reedmedia.eu/contact as an example. Instead of a static map, visitors can zoom in and out, find directions, use Google Streetview where available, and even review your business! Even if you don't put a map on your site, it's worth listing your business in Google Maps, especially if you are a local business. It's free, and another way for people to find you.

These third-party web tools, and others like them, enable you to offer a much wider range of services than you could yourself. The subscription fees involved are modest compared to the time and money you would spend on building your own web functions – and some are free. Don't worry about looking 'unprofessional' if you use these services – they are commonly used by even the biggest brands. Their level of specialism and ease of use makes these tools compelling, and provide a better experience for your customers than you could build yourself.

Get social: build connections and community

Dynamic, changing content will make you look more up to date, and more popular with search engines. Compelling content will keep people coming back for more. Third-party tools will extend your functions. But to really engage your clients and customers, you need to go where they are and start conversations with them.

> **❝ compelling content will keep people coming back for more ❞**

In the relatively recent old days of 'Web 1.0', businesses would put all their online marketing efforts into their website – if they even had one. Now this is an area where the 80/20 rule applies. Only 20 per cent of your online marketing time should be spent on your core business website. The other 80 per cent should be spent on your blog, your Facebook page, your Twitter feed, and other social sites. It should be spent connecting with people, creating community, and raising awareness of your brand. This 'off site' activity will draw people on to your website – but it is far more productive to engage with people there than on your own site.

This is what makes your website a marketing hub: at the centre of the spokes that lead out to a variety of social sites. Spend time building your site, getting it right, and making sure it has all the key functions you need to do business – and keep it up to date – but then get out there, get social, and grow your business!

Measure your results

Website analytics

Your web stats, or web analytics, are the primary means by which you will measure the effectiveness of your website. All services available run on the same principle: you sign up for an account, tell it which website(s) you want to track, and it gives you some code to include on all the pages you want it to track. This is usually a simple matter of adding the code to your 'footer' file and uploading it.

Google Analytics (www.google.com/analytics) This is the most popular service, used on around 40 per cent of the 10,000 most popular websites. It is free to use for up to 50 sites – so long as each site has fewer than five million page views per month or is linked to an AdWords campaign (see next chapter). It has great analytical tools and reports, detailing a wealth of information about site visitors. It also integrates nicely with AdWords campaigns, and helps you analyse the effectiveness of your landing pages and conversions from your Google ads.

Clicky Analytics (www.getclicky.com) This is free to use for up to three sites, and then there are payment plans for up to 10, 30 or 100 sites, with their 'Pro' account (up to 10 sites / $60 or about £40 per year) being the most popular. It offers many of the same services as Google Analytics, but in real time, and provides details on every action by every visitor. I also like Clicky because it tracks traffic from around 60 social sites, and it will also keep track of the number of your RSS feed subscribers (through Feedburner) and track Twitter searches, all from the same dashboard.

Website rankings

You can also measure where your site ranks by signing up to Alexa (www.alexa.com) or the Google Toolbar, which includes the Google PageRank bar. You can also look at the rankings for any website – including your competitors.

Alexa Internet This is the web traffic and ranking site that is a subsidiary of Amazon.com. Download their toolbar from www.alexa.com/toolbar. Once installed, the toolbar collects data on browsing behaviour which is sent back to the website where it is stored and analysed and is the basis for their web traffic reporting. You can use the toolbar to see how popular a website is, how many sites are linking to it, find sites that are similar to it, and even how it looked in the past using it's 'Wayback' feature. You can also see what the hot pages and searches are on the Internet right now. Alexa rankings are often quoted to illustrate how popular a website is – for example, at the time of writing, Facebook has an Alexa ranking of 2 (i.e. the second most popular website in the world), YouTube 3 and Twitter 11. (You see why it's a good idea to be visible on these sites?)

PageRank Is the Google algorithm that expresses Google's view of the importance of a particular webpage as a score out of 10, and is partly determined by the number of incoming links. Google interprets a link from page A to page B as a 'vote' for page B. But the strength of that vote also depends on how important Google considers page A to be. We will look more at page rankings in the next chapter.

Inbound links

You can get a measure of your incoming links from your web stats and Alexa, and also use your web stats to see what search terms people are using to find you. In addition, you can use a free tool from HubSpot called Website Grader (http://websitegrader.com) to gain insights into how many inbound links you have, how many of your pages are indexed by Google, and suggestions for improving your website. You can also compare your data with those of your competition!

Take action

■ **Secure** a domain name for your business.

■ **Decide** whether to hire a designer or do it yourself.

■ **Set up** your business website.

■ **Plan** your design brief and content.

■ **Extend** your functionality with third-party sites.

■ **Focus** on building connections and community on social sites.

Boost your search engine rankings

How to increase your visibility on Google

N
ow that you've built your website, people won't necessarily come. Not if they can't find you. And the main way people find you online is still via search engines. Without a website, you don't exist. Without a search strategy, you exist but you're invisible. Google isn't the only search engine – others are available, including Yahoo!, Bing and Ask. But Google is so big it has become a verb – and has a market share of over 70 per cent as of February 2010. Nor is Google the only way people search for what they want online. People also search on Facebook, Twitter, YouTube and other social sites they spend so much time on. Much of the rest of this book will help you to be found on these sites too, but being on these sites will also make you more visible on Google.

without a search strategy, you exist but you're invisible

People also discover sites through 'social search', using sites like Delicious, Digg and StumbleUpon, where it is people rather than machines and algorithms who decide which are the best sites and items of content by ranking, rating and sharing them. We will look more at social search and social bookmarking in Chapter 15. The principles in this chapter apply to all search engines, but we will pay particular attention to improving your visibility in Google.

What is search engine marketing?

How Google works

Google is the world's largest search engine. It does two things:

1 Crawls the Internet looking for web pages, and indexes them in a vast catalogue. It is no longer necessary to manually submit websites to Google – it happens automatically. Google will find your pages via incoming links from websites that are already indexed. This is one reason why you want other sites to link to yours. You can also manually submit your site at www.google.com/addurl if you want. This is the easy part.

2 Decides which are the best pages – both the best match for a search query, and the ones that have the best rank. Getting your pages to rank highly is the harder part, and is what search engine marketing (SEM) will achieve for you.

The decision-making algorithm that decides which pages are the best is based on two things: relevance and authority. The relevance of a page to the search query is simply based on the key words used to perform a search. But since there are likely to be hundreds of thousands of pages that match, Google then ranks them in order of authority, using its PageRank algorithm.

This algorithm is based on work done at Stanford University on how to measure the authority of academic papers. The simple answer is: citations. The more a paper is cited by other papers, the more authority it has. But not all citations are equal: a citation from a paper that itself has a lot of citations carries more weight that a citation from one that has few or none.

This is exactly how the Google PageRank algorithm works. The more links there are from other websites to your website, the more authority your website has. But not all incoming links are equal: an incoming link from a website that itself has a lot of incoming links carries more weight than an incoming link from one that has few or none.

How search engine marketing works

Online marketing is all about making your stuff easy to find. Search engine marketing (SEM) is about making your stuff easy to find on Google and other search engines, by increasing the position of your placement on search engine results pages (SERPs). This is done via three methods:

1   Search engine optimisation (SEO) – making your website more attractive to Google

2   Paid placements – e.g. using Google AdWords

3   Attracting in-bound links – e.g. using article marketing.

The good news is that the first of these methods – SEO – is not only free but also more effective. If you can increase your natural or organic search engine rankings, i.e. without paying for them, people are more likely to click on them. Research shows that 75 per cent of people using Google click on the natural search results, and 25 per cent on the paid-for ads.

Google AdWords is still worth a look, though, and needn't cost a fortune. Your paid-for listings become cheaper and more effective the more specific to your business the search terms you choose are. Search engine marketing is affordable even for small businesses.

Part of the aim of your SEM is to get incoming links from high-authority sites, in order to increase your authority and therefore your position on SERPs. We will therefore also take a look at article marketing in this chapter. This involves submitting content to high-ranking article sites such as Ezine (http://ezinearticles.com) in order to drive traffic back to your site and increase your credibility by positioning you as an expert in your field – but also to increase your authority with Google.

Like so much in the online marketing world, one of the best ways to encourage links to your website is to create great content. The content tools we will look at in Part 3 will help you create content for your website and for other social sites. Blogs in particular really help push up your search engine rankings. Of course, creating a remarkable business – what Seth Godin calls a *Purple Cow* – helps too!

> **blogs in particular really help push up your search engine rankings**

Why search engine marketing works for business

How many times have you looked for something on Google today? How many other people out there are searching right now for products or services exactly like the ones you offer? How many will find your website? Most people – about 90 per cent – don't get past page 1 of the search engine results delivered by Google. Getting a high placement on this page is critical to driving search engine traffic to your site.

A high placement can be paid for (though Google still selects the results it thinks will be most appropriate to the person searching, to maintain its own credibility), or achieved for free through SEO and getting links from high-authority sites.

For example, if you've just launched your website for your catering business and no one is linking to it yet, Google assigns a low authority to your pages. If you then start a blog, each post is a new page for Google to index. Food bloggers may find you and start linking to your blog posts. This will increase your authority and your position on Google. Then if a site such as the *Observer Food Monthly* website happens to have links to your site, your authority will skyrocket, since this site is a high-rankiJigsawng website with lots of incoming links.

Google is a global site, but your business doesn't have to be global to benefit from it. People can choose to restrict search results to their own country for a start. But what if you're really local, and only really serve your local community? What if you're, say, a plumber who wants to focus on local work in your own town and the surrounding area? The traditional marketing approach would be to advertise in the local paper, and perhaps print leaflets and go out putting them through your neighbours' doors.

❝ Google is a global site, but your business doesn't have to be global to benefit from it ❞

But a plumber is the sort of service you only need when you need it – it is not an impulse purchase. This means that you have to do repeat advertising every week in the local paper, and regular leaflet drops in order to get your phone number in front of your potential customers when they need you. That's going to be expensive.

If instead you have a website, people can Google you – the first port of call for many of us when we need a service. Make sure the locations you serve are on your website, so that searches for 'plumber Oxford' (or wherever) come up. Google's maps and local business service make this even easier. If I simply search for 'plumber', Google supplies the page shown in Figure 4.1.

Now, there are almost 10 million results for such a common word, as you might expect. But Google has learned that I live in Woking, and has supplied the top seven search results nearest to me, and shown them on an interactive map. For this reason, if you are a local business you *must* list yourself in what Google calls its 'Local Business Center'. It's free to do this at www.google.com/local/add.

figure 4.1 Google search engine results page

Note that the top three search results, with shading behind them, and the eight results in the right-hand column, are paid-for Google Ads. This is indicated by the heading 'Sponsored Links'. The rest are natural, or organic, search results. Unsurprisingly a Wikipedia definition is top of this list, since Wikipedia is such a high-authority site with lots of incoming links.

search engine marketing in action

All Jigsaw Puzzles (www.alljigsawpuzzles.co.uk)

Starting from his back bedroom in 2001, Alan Maclachlan's passion for jigsaws has turned his business World Ideas Ltd into the UK's largest online supplier of jigsaws. Still a small family-run business, he nonetheless took their 200,000th order just before Christmas 2009 via his www.alljigsawpuzzles.co.uk website – one of several he runs. Type the very common word 'jigsaws' into Google, and this website is likely to be at the top of the natural search results in the UK.

Both Google AdWords and natural search results form the basis of the company's marketing strategy. Keywords are searched for using the Google AdWords

> keyword tool, and they also use SEO techniques to make sure they are at the top of the natural search results. Alan says: 'People who are already searching a product are halfway to committing to buy.'
>
> The company also aims for high-ranking websites to link back to their websites. This helps build authority and boosts rankings. They send articles to Ezine about once a week on a range of topics, of around 250–400 words each, all of which include their keywords in the title and two or three times throughout an article. They also include a clickable link in the author resource box at the end of each article back to the World Ideas site they are promoting. The effectiveness of this strategy can be measured, since Ezine give statistics on how many people view each article and click through from it. Alan and his team also submit articles to articlealley.com and articlebase.com. The team also use a blog, a newsletter and video to raise the profile of their websites.
>
> Perhaps the most intriguing way World Ideas use search engines is for product development. They search for new products using the Google keyword tool, as well as drawing inspiration from visiting other websites and high street stores. They then look to see how many search results there have been for particular terms and the competition for the keywords. That's really putting the Google horse before the shopping cart – finding out what products people are searching for, and *then* developing them – and a great way to generate new product ideas.
>
> **Get the idea**: Use search engine optimisation, Google AdWords and article marketing in combination for best results. Use the Google Keyword Tool (www.google.com/sktool) to improve your Google AdWords campaigns but also to generate ideas for new products to develop.

Get up to speed with search engine marketing

There are three things you can do to get your SEM off to a great start:

1 Optimise your website.
2 Create a Google AdWords campaign.
3 Submit an article to Ezine.

Optimise your website

Get a natural high for your search results, for free, simply by taking a bit of time to make sure your website is as optimised as possible for search engines. SEO had a bad name in the early days of the Web, when it was too often thought of as tricking Google into giving you a high ranking.

Well, Google is wise to that now, and will soon boot you off if you try any of those 'black hat' techniques such as hiding keywords invisibly on your website. Besides, that's not very authentic, is it? And you don't want traffic simply because you're top of the Google list – you want it because what you have to offer is *relevant* to what people are searching for. Google delivers the results that are the best match for its searchers, and you get visitors who are actually interested in buying from you. It's a win–win situation.

The first step is to make sure your website contains the right content and code for Google to know that your site is relevant to people searching on certain keywords. Things to pay attention to are:

- **Page titles** – give each page its own title.
- **Page descriptions** – these show up in Google search results rather than on your site, and provide more information about your site.
- **URLs** – make sure they include keywords. Blogs are great for this as the title of the blogpost usually shows up in the URL.
- **Website content** – think about the headings you use, the text you use as links (choose something descriptive rather than 'click here'), and tag your images with text that is visible to Google (but not to your visitors), so that it can 'see' them.

Find out more about optimising your site for search engines at www.getuptospeed.biz/seo.

Create a Google AdWords campaign

Google AdWords is an example of pay per click (PPC) advertising. Each time someone clicks on one of your ads that shows up on the 'Sponsored Links' section of the Google results page, you pay a small fee. You may prefer to focus on boosting your natural search results for free with SEO. But it's worth trying Google AdWords, if only for short periods of time, particularly when you first launch your website and have no traffic, or whenever you launch a new product or service that you want to raise awareness of.

Sign up for an account at http://adwords.google.com, and start creating your first campaign. Choose your ad text, the keywords you want to target (i.e. which search queries do you want Google to display your ad in response to?), and decide what your maximum bid is for those key-words. You can choose how much you pay, and set a daily budget, but bear in mind that the whole system is a live auction, and someone may outbid you for a higher place, particularly with very popular, generic – and expensive – keywords. It is also possible that a keyword will suddenly become more popular, and the cost per click (CPC) will go up.

It makes sense to try to stick to more niche, specific keywords in your campaign for two reasons:

1 It's more effective – you will get more targeted traffic.
2 It's cheaper – common search terms are more expensive.

You get a very limited number of words for your ad – so choose them carefully! You can also set up multiple variations of the same ad, and test them against each other – Google will help you pick the best one with the metrics it provides.

You can also send people who click on your ad to a specific landing page, so you can measure its effectiveness. The URL doesn't have to match the home page URL shown on the ad – though it must be the same domain. For example, if someone clicks on the 'Confused by Social Media?' heading in the ad below, they click through to www.reedmedia.eu/workshops. I could equally have used a unique landing page that was only used for that specific ad.

> Confused by **Social Media?**
> Learn how to market your business
> with **social media** on our **workshop**
> www.reedmedia.eu
> London

figure 4.2 Google ad

In addition to textual ads, you can also opt for image ads in a variety of standard sizes, and even video ads.

The ads you create don't just show up in Google either. The flipside of Google AdWords is Google AdSense. That is an ad-serving service that enables anyone with a blog or website to earn a bit of cash by hosting contextually relevant Google ads on their pages. So your ads could show up on a wide variety of other sites too.

Choosing keywords

Think about what search terms people will use to find you, and include them in your AdWords campaign – as well as on your website. Most people take the products and services they offer as a starting point, and think of all the keywords and search terms associated with them, and then generate a list to use within the text of their website.

But the other way you can do this is to research the search terms people most often use in relation to your product or service. One way of doing this is to enter your web address into the Google search-based keyword tool at www.google.com/sktool.

> **❝ research the search terms people most often use ❞**

This will come up with keyword suggestions for you, based on pairing the content on all your pages with actual search terms that people use on Google. It will output a list of keywords in order of search volume: an instant, up-to-date keyword list customised to your site.

You don't need to be logged in to AdWords to use this service – but if you are, you can incorporate any keywords from the suggested list right into your AdWords campaign.

For example, the Google search-based keyword tool revealed that some of the high-volume search terms I wasn't using for my www.smallbusiness studio.co.uk site related to business card designs and stationery. This is one of the services I offer through that site, but the service that is searched for more than any other. As well as giving me some ideas for tweaking my web copy and Google Ads, this also suggests I should per-haps focus more on that offering as part of the business, and/or use it as a way to draw people on to the site and up-sell other services. You can use research into search terms not only as a way of developing your web copy and Google Ads – but also as a way of developing your business.

Keyword ideas for (English, United Kingdom) edit

Save to draft　Export ▼

Keyword	Monthly searches ↓	Competition	Sugg. bid	Ad/Search share	Extracted from web page
New keywords related to smallbusinessstudio.co.uk (258) Keywords not already in your account					
business card printing	3,500		£2.33	0% / 0%	Pricing | Small Business Studio
business card design	1,800		£1.87	0% / 0%	Pricing | Small Business Studio
design a logo	1,200		£0.66	0% / 0%	Pricing | Small Business Studio
print business cards	1,000		£1.98	0% / 0%	Pricing | Small Business Studio
business card designs	820		£1.68	0% / 0%	Pricing | Small Business Studio
business cards printing	820		£2.29	0% / 0%	Pricing | Small Business Studio
business card printers	820		£2.46	0% / 0%	Pricing | Small Business Studio
compliment slips	820		£0.93	0% / 0%	Pricing | Small Business Studio
web design packages	660		£3.28	0% / 0%	Web Design | Small Business Studio

figure 4.3　Google keyword tool

Once your website is up and running, another thing you can do is to look at your web stats to see what search terms people are using to find you – and then tweak your keywords if it seems appropriate.

Note that this keyword research can also help you improve your web copy, titles, descriptions and headings, plus suggest topics to blog about, all of which will improve your natural search results without costing you a penny.

Submit an article to Ezine

Part of your SEM strategy is to get more incoming links from high-ranking websites. One way to do this is to create great content that people will not only find via search and social media, but will also want to link to. You *can* also ask people to link to you – but I would advise against this. I get link requests all the time, mostly from people who haven't understood what I do. I treat them as spam and delete them.

One way you might think you can create incoming links to your website is to comment on other people's blogs – particularly if they are high-ranking blogs or news sites – since you can usually enter your URL with your comment. While this can indeed be great for driving traffic to your website, I'm afraid it doesn't work for boosting your site's authority in Google's eyes. These links are not, after all, citations of your website by an independent third party, as PageRank intended – and Google is wise to it. To get around this issue, the 'no-follow' attribute for certain links was invented. When Google sees a 'no-follow' link, it knows that the site owner doesn't want to endorse the site being linked to. This applies to most blogs.

An exception to this is article sites such as Ezine (http://ezinearticles.com) – sites that you can submit content to with a by-line and a biography box with a ('do-follow') link back to your website. Ezine is a high-authority site, and links back to your site will increase your authority. People reproduce Ezine articles on their own blogs and websites – on the condition that they are reproduced in full with full credit to the author complete with byline, bio and link – so Ezine is used by both content creators and consumers.

A note of caution, though: please don't use these sites cynically by putting up poor-quality articles with links. They are not just about link-building, and they shouldn't be thought of as an acceptable face of the old 'black hat' technique of link farms: they are also about sharing your knowledge, building your credibility and positioning you as an expert. Like blog comments, you should expect to get traffic as a result. Unlike blog comments, you will also get SEO credit for the links.

Use social media to increase search engine placements

A blog is one of the best ways of increasing your search engine results: you create more pages for Google to index, and more content that people will want to link to (see Chapter 6). But since other social sites, such as Twitter and Facebook are themselves high-ranking sites, why not create accounts for your business? If you can gain at least 25 Facebook fans, and if it's available, you can even have your own URL – such as www.facebook.com/publishingtalk. For me, this and the Twitter account http://twitter.com/publishingtalk are higher results for the search query 'publishing talk' in Google than the www.publishingtalk.eu site itself.

Don't underestimate the power of social media to help you to be found – not just on social media sites themselves, but within Google. Having a presence on social sites help people to find your business – even if they don't use these sites themselves.

Measure your results

One way to measure the results of your SEM campaign is simply to look at your web stats and measure your web traffic. But your traffic is not entirely generated by Google – especially if you are using social media to drive people to your website – so you will need to dig a bit deeper into the stats.

■ You also get a load of stats and metrics with Google AdWords to help you find out what's working and what isn't, and to help you improve your campaigns. If you use unique landing pages with your Google ads, you can also work out not only how much traffic is coming from your ads (which Google will tell you), but also how many visitors are converting into leads.

■ Search Google yourself, using some of your chosen keywords, and note your natural search engine placements. If you're not coming as high up the list as you'd like, do something about it.

■ You can also search Google for just the pages in your site, by entering 'site:mybusiness.com'. This will tell you how many pages of your site are indexed by Google – and which pages have the highest authority, since these appear top of the list.

■ Finally, monitor the number of incoming links to your website. Part of your SEM strategy is to increase the number and quality of these, so this is something you should be vigilant about.

Take action

▪ Optimise your website for Google.

▪ List your business in the Google Local Business Center at www.google.com/local/add.

▪ Research your keywords with www.google.com/sktool.

▪ Sign up to Google AdWords and start your first campaign.

▪ Submit an article to Ezine.

5

Engage with email

How to build an email list without annoying people

The word 'spam', to mean unwanted junk email, derives from the Monty Python sketch of the same name. If you think email marketing involves sending people unsolicited Viagra ads, think again. Email is a tried and tested method for reaching the right people online *and* persuading them to take action.

You need very little technical knowledge to get started, since there are plenty of excellent third-party services you can use, such as MailChimp or Campaign Monitor, to handle everything from sign-up forms and email templates to managing mailing lists and measuring your results. This allows you to focus instead on your email marketing strategy: your marketing aims, who you will target, and what you will email them.

What is email marketing?

Email marketing is the online equivalent of direct mail. Although every email you send to a client or potential customer could be thought of as email marketing, it really means sending bulk emails to your email list, or part of your list, with aims that might include:

- **Building** your relationship with existing customers.
- **Encouraging** repeat business.
- **Acquiring** new customers.
- **Persuading** people to buy something.

When it is used *with permission* for building and maintaining relationships with your customers, email marketing is an efficient and powerful tool that needs to be part of your online marketing mix.

Why email marketing works for business

'Why bother with email in the social media age?', you may ask. 'I've built up a massive opted-in mailing list on Facebook and Twitter – can't I just use that?' Well, yes, that is one of your aims for using social sites. And if you haven't yet built up a following, you'll find out how to in Chapters 10–13.

But there are three important reasons why email is still central to your online marketing even if you market your business on social networks:

1 **You own the data.** What happens if you get booted off Facebook, or if Twitter goes down at a critical moment? What if the entire social network you've been relying on goes under? If you've built up your own email list, this isn't a problem, as you, rather than a third-party site, own the data. Yes, build up your following on social networks – but also try to convert them to your mailing list subscribers.

2 **It is a more appropriate sales channel.** Not everyone likes being sold to on social networks. You need to use them with caution, keep your message relevant, and not just spam a social network with 'buy my product' messages. We're much more used to email as a sales channel, however, and if we've given permission to be included on an email list, we expect to be sold to at least some of the time.

3 **Not everyone uses a social networking site.** And those who do don't necessarily log on every day. However, most people pick up their email every day.

One of your key calls to action on the social media channels you use should be 'Sign up to our newsletter'.

---

email marketing in action

Stills (www.stills.org)

Stills is a small Edinburgh-based visual art gallery dedicated to exhibiting contemporary photography. As well as exhibitions, talks and events, they also provide facilities such as darkrooms and equipment hire, and offer training courses. Established over 30 years ago, they have more recently used online marketing, and seen dramatic results – particularly with email marketing, which has resulted in a massive jump in sales and increase in attendance.

▶

▶ Stills previously relied on direct mail, and supplemented this by sending hand-crafted emails to a subset of their physical mailing list. In 2007 they switched to a professional email service provider (ESP) – and saw the results from the moment they sent their first e-flyer. They now send two e-flyers per month to a growing list of over 4,000 subscribers, where previously they sent only four a year to less than 2,000 people. Generally, one e-flyer is about exhibitions, the other about courses. Using an ESP means they can easily ask people at sign-up which sort of e-flyer they're interested in receiving, and send e-flyers to subsets of their main list. They have recently switched to MailChimp as their ESP, since online sales of courses, space and exhibition publications are becoming more important, and MailChimp integrates nicely with other third-party services such as PayPal.

Stills built their list primarily through their website, by making 'Join our mailing list' a prominent call to action. The website already received a lot of traffic, so this was a key driver of sign-ups.

The organisation can have a closer relationship with its core user base by using email and social media. Stills's Development Manager, Carrie Maginn says: 'Marketing is not just about giving information out – it is about listening and responding. It's a dialogue, not a monologue. And that's a lot more fun and more rewarding.'

Stills have also been using social media since 2009, particularly Flickr, Blipfoto and YouTube for content, and Facebook and Twitter for outreach. Facebook is used to promote events, and time-limited incentives appear on Twitter, such as 'DM us by 2pm today for a free darkroom session'. Importantly, social media supports and enhances their email marketing, since an exhibition or course will be simultaneously promoted by email, on the website and on Facebook and Twitter. This encourages word of mouth marketing which, along with email, is their biggest driver of sales.

Carrie says: 'Whether you like it or not, you've got to use online marketing. In the current climate there is no money – and this is free. If you invest time in understanding it and its benefits, and do it well, the ROI is there – you can see it.'

Get the idea: Use a professional ESP to grow your list. Use MailChip to integrate with other software such as PayPal. You can even segment your MailChimp lists by purchase activity using their E-Commerce 360 plugin (www.mailchimp .com/plugins/e-commerce-360), which integrates with Magneto, PrestaShop, osCommerce and ZenCart e-commerce software. You know how Amazon send you up-selling emails saying 'If you liked X you might also like Y'? You too can do that by integrating your ESP with other software.

Get up to speed with email marketing

1 Choose an email service provider (ESP).

2 Build your list.

3 Plan your campaign.

4 Write your first email.

Choose an email service provider

Don't even think about using your own email account to send mass mailings. For one thing, it only takes a low percentage of people to classify your mail as junk to give you real problems, possibly including suspension of your email account. A professional email service provider (ESP) will help you comply with legal requirements, since they generally adopt best practices, such as double-opt in systems and 'unsubscribe' links in each email footer. These services will also help you manage and maintain your email list database, including enabling you to split it into segments for highly targeted campaigns. But the other huge advantage is the detailed reporting statistics that they provide, which would be almost impossible for you to replicate in-house. These include how many people have opened your email, and how many have clicked through to specific links you included in your email.

❝ don't even think about using your own email account to send mass mailings ❞

Popular ESPs include:

- Campaign Monitor (www.campaignmonitor.com)
- Dotmailer (www.dotmailer.com)
- Emma (www.myemma.com)
- MailChimp (www.mailchimp.com)
- Short Burst (www.shortburst.co.uk).

These services all work in a similar way:

1 Upload your email contact list if you have one already, and manage your lists and sublists via the service.

2 Create an email newsletter sign-up form – usually a simple matter of choosing which fields you want to include – then copy the code provided and paste it into your website or blog. People who sign

up using this form will be added to your mailing list. Most services will also allow you to customise the 'Thank you for signing up to our mailing list' messages, including the emails that go out asking people to confirm their subscription if you choose a double opt-in system. You can also use these confirmation messages to include a link to, say, a free downloadable resource that you offered as an incentive for signing up. Other 'autoresponders' are often available too. For example, to automatically send a message a specific time after someone has signed up.

3   Choose a ready-made email template or design your own. The amount of customisation available varies with each ESP.

4   Create a 'campaign' – i.e. a specific mailing. Write your email, test it by sending to yourself, then send it to one of your lists or sublists.

5   Measure your results. Whichever service you choose will provide detailed metrics on who has received, opened, taken action and clicked through to specific links within your email.

Build your list

Now that you've got a service provider, complete with a database to hold all those email addresses, how are you going to populate it? I would advise against buying in a list. Apart from risking contravening the increasingly strict laws about email marketing, it is cheaper and more effective to build your own. Email marketing should be about building relationships with people who actually want to hear from you.

Get permission The overriding principle is you MUST get permission. Effective email marketing is permissions-based marketing – not spam. If someone signs up to your list, they know to expect email from you. They are more likely to be interested in your email, and it is less likely to end up in their spam folder. Ideally, use a double opt-in system. This sends an email to someone who has signed up to your newsletter asking them to click on a link to confirm their subscription.

Create a sign-up form This is very easy – no knowledge of HTML is required. Whichever email marketing service you use, a standard feature is the generation of an email newsletter sign-up form that you can put on your website or blog. Just choose the fields you want, and copy and paste the code.

Make 'Sign up to our newsletter' your number one call to action Your email newsletter sign-up form is the most important call to action on your website, and should be in a prominent position on your home page, your newsletter page if you have one, and ideally on other key pages. But you can also use it as a call to action in any form of online marketing you use, including on your blog, your podcast, and on Twitter, Facebook and LinkedIn.

Offer an incentive Create a white paper, a short ebook or other downloadable resource that your community will value. Give it away for free – or, rather, sell it for the price of an email address. This can be an effective way of kick-starting your list, since there are many other channels through which you can market your free resource – such as your Twitter, Facebook or LinkedIn lists, on your website, and using Google AdWords.

Ask in person Whenever you take a business card from someone, whether a prospective client, someone you meet at a networking event, conference or trade show, ask them if you can add them to your newsletter. You can sign them up manually to your list so long as you have their permission. And if you use a double opt-in system, they can always change their mind.

Provide an example To show prospective subscribers exactly what they are signing up to, include a link to your latest newsletter, or include an image of it on your newsletter page.

Plan your campaign

As with all of your marketing activities, decide on your objectives. Selling might be one of them – but it is not the only thing email marketing can be used for. Some of your emails may not be directly sales-related, but draw people on to your website or promote your products or services more indirectly. Your content and style may vary accordingly.

A 'campaign' in email marketing usually means a specific, single mailing. But it can also be used to describe your overall approach over a longer period of time. Types of email you might send include:

Special offers A very common way to use email marketing, and an incentive for people to sign up to your list, is to make promotional offers available exclusively to subscribers. Use time-limited discount codes, and measure responses with click-throughs (as measured by your email marketing service), unique landing pages (as measured by your web stats) or simply by using a unique discount code for each campaign.

Quick announcements Sometimes called postcard emails, these are brief announcements with a single call to action that might relate to a time-restricted sale or special offer.

Customer surveys Surveys can be used to gain feedback on your service, or help develop new products (while at the same time raising awareness of your new product). They are easy to set up using www.surveymonkey.com, which also allows you to import an emailing list and manage responses – for example by sending a follow-up email only to those who haven't yet replied. Although your branding options are limited, the 'from' field can be any email address you specify. Use the same email address you use for your normal marketing emails to maintain trust. Alternatively, you can send out a regular email to your list with a link to your survey; you just won't be able to send follow-ups to people who haven't completed it.

Press releases If you have a discrete list of media contacts you've built up, this can be a useful way of distributing press releases with a view to getting media coverage. Include links to the virtual press room on your website.

Newsletters Possibly the most common form of email marketing is a regular newsletter that is sent to your entire list. An email newsletter is a 'softer' way of selling. It can be a powerful way of keeping in touch with your clients and customers without annoying them with constant sales messages. The purpose of an email newsletter is relationship building with previous, current and prospective clients. The focus is on providing useful information in their niche field of interest – a similar approach that you would adopt with a blog (see Chapter 6). You might even include some extracts from latest blog posts with a 'read more...' link, in order to draw them on to your site. While the information is related to what you can offer, it is not a hard sell. It should, however, include a call to action.

Your newsletter may contain some or all of these:

- Useful information about your area of expertise.
- Latest news from your industry.
- Tips and 'how to' features.
- Upcoming events, conferences or trade fairs you will be attending.
- Special offers with discount codes exclusive to subscribers.
- Details of a new product you've launched and the key benefits it offers.

Write your first email

Keep your messages short and to the point, compelling, interesting and valuable. Make sure they are personalised, relevant to the list or subsection of the list you are sending it to, get the right message to the right person, and include a call to action. If you have several sections in your newsletter, consider using extracts and 'read more…' links to direct them to the full article on your blog or website. Think carefully about the individual elements of your emails, particularly:

■ **From.** Send email from a person. It is more likely to be opened if the email address is recognised as a real person by the recipient, ideally from someone they are already used to receiving email from. This is easy to configure, whichever service you use. Just specify the 'from' address you want.

■ **Subject.** Grab attention, but avoid any words that might get trapped by a spam filter. These includes 'FREE!'

■ **To.** As with your 'from' field, all the emails in your database should be to a real person. Your email is unlikely to reach anyone if it is being sent to info@, sales@, etc.

■ **Body.** The general rule for HTML emails is a maximum width of 600px, but your ESP should handle any formatting, size and layout requirements. When it comes to composing your email, keep the information in short, bite-sized chunks with the most important information at the top of your email.

■ **Call to action.** Don't confuse people with too many calls to action. If you can include one clear prominent call to action in each newsletter – perhaps a 'buy now' button, or a link to 'read more', 'take our survey', 'subscribe to our podcast' or whatever it may be – you are more likely to get click-throughs.

■ **Footer.** Always be clear about how recipients can unsubscribe and put in all your contact information so people can get in touch with you, and to meet any statutory requirements. The UK, for example, requires businesses to include their registered address and number on websites and emails as well as printed stationery.

Always send yourself a test email before mailing your entire list to make sure it looks as you intended and there are no glaring errors or omissions.

Use FeedBurner to create an email newsletter from your blog

If you have a blog, it automatically comes with an RSS feed. That stands for 'Really Simple Syndication', and is simply a way for people to subscribe to your latest blog posts in a newsreader such as Google Reader. But if you manage your feed through a free service called www.feedburner.com you have additional options for the way you deliver your blog feed – including delivering latest posts by email. This means you can set up an ad-hoc email newsletter from your blog if you're not yet ready to take the plunge with MailChimp, Campaign Monitor or one of the other professional email marketing services.

■ Create a separate 'newsletter' category within your blog (which will generate its own RSS feed) – or consider your entire blog your newsletter.

■ Use FeedBurner to create a feed – for your blog or for the discrete newsletter category you created.

■ On the FeedBurner site, click on the **Publicize** tab and then the **Email Subscriptions** link in the left-hand menu.

■ Two alternative pieces of HTML code are supplied: a sign-up form or a simple link. Use this on your blog or website.

■ Click the **Email Branding** link to choose the text and link colours your email will use, and the logo you want to appear on it.

■ To see the email addresses of people who have subscribed to your RSS feed by email, click the **Analyze** tab and the **See more about your subscribers** link. Scroll down, beneath the pie chart, to **Email Subscription Services**. Click on **FeedBurner Email Subscriptions** and then **Manage Your Email Subscribers List**. You will see a list of email addresses of people who have subscribed to your RSS feed. You can export these if you wish.

The advantages of this approach, if you already have a blog, is that it is an incredibly easy way to set up an email newsletter. The downside is that, although you have access to the list of email addresses, you can't send a message to them without creating a new blog post. This means you can't make special offers available to subscribers only – since everyone can see your newsletter on your blog. You also don't have access to the metrics you have with an email marketing service. This is really just an alternative way of delivering your latest blog posts to those who prefer to receive them by email instead of visiting your site. But it can be a useful halfway house between a blog and a newsletter. It is certainly a great way of promoting your blog.

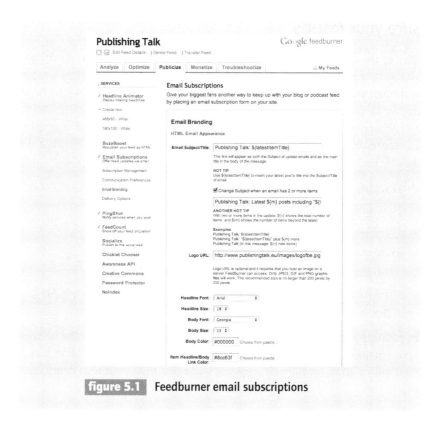

Manage the workload

Plan your emails in advance, and consider theming them around specific topics, products or services and tying them into other areas of your online marketing such as the schedule for your blog or podcast. This will help you stay focused on specific promotions you want to do throughout the year, and help you repurpose material. Include extracts from your latest blog posts with 'read more…' links to lead them back on to your site.

Consider getting some help with your email marketing. A virtual assistant or other outsourced professional can help you create email templates, write copy and manage your lists. There are plenty of people who are very experienced with all the major ESPs such as MailChimp and Campaign Monitor. See Chapter 16 for advice on finding someone.

Measure your results

One of the many advantages of using a professional email marketing service is that it comes with a wide range of stats and metrics. Most people will open your email – if they're going to – within a few days, so the feedback you get on your campaign (i.e. a single emailing) is fairly quick. Many services will present the information as pie charts or other graphical representations, in a sophisticated amount of detail. Information usually includes:

- How many people opened your email.
- How many bounced.
- How many people classed you as spam.
- Who clicked on to your website from the email.
- Who clicked on specific links within your email.
- Which email clients your subscribers used, e.g. Outlook, Apple Mail, iPhone.

In addition, if you used any unique landing pages and URLs in the links in your emails, you will be able to track these via your web stats. All of this is vital information for following up leads and planning your next campaign.

Take action

- **Choose** an email service provider (ESP).
- **Build** your email list, making sure to add a sign-up form to your website.
- **Plan** your email marketing strategy.
- **Create** an engaging newsletter that provides value to your customers.
- **Compose** your first email and measure the results of your campaign.

three

Get creative

Build a blog

How to build trust, reputation and traffic

According to *The Cluetrain Manifesto* (www.cluetrain.com), all markets are conversations. A blog is a great way to start a conversation. It is also your key content tool – and content is the starting point for the value you will add to your marketing activities. Yes, you want to get the word out about your product or service. But social media is also about creating genuinely valuable content that your community will appreciate and want to share. You need to create value – not just ask people to buy from you.

A blog can be the hub of your social media. You can use it to aggregate other media, by including images, video and audio as well as text. You can pull in feeds from other websites, such as your Twitter updates or your Flickr photos. And you can create feeds so that people can subscribe to your latest content. A blog is also the easiest way to set up a website: you can even use one as your main business site.

> a blog is also the easiest way to set up a website

What is a blog?

A blog, short for 'web log', is a kind of online diary. The author writes entries, or 'posts' which have a date attached, and appear in reverse chronological order – i.e. with the newest entry at the top. Pages can be added as well as posts, via a simple to use content management system. Blogs started as personal journals, but have evolved into something far more powerful, and useful, for business.

There are a number of features of blogs that make them different from an ordinary, static website.

1 **Sidebar.** A blog will usually have one or two sidebars – a column or two, usually on the right hand side of the main part of the screen where your posts appear. This includes extra information such as your blogroll (see below), and links to latest posts and comments.

2 **Categories.** Posts are usually organised into categories to help people browse your content by topic.

3 **Tags.** These are keywords attached to individual posts, and another way to navigate to the content that your readers are interested in. Many blogs include a 'tag cloud' in the sidebar, which displays the most commonly used tags in different font sizes, with the largest being more popular.

4 **Comments.** Readers can usually write their own comments on your posts, below what you've written. Comments will usually include the commenter's name, and link back to their own website or blog. This makes blogs a social medium – a two-way conversation and a forum for discussion and feedback, rather than a broadcast. Comments can be moderated before they go live.

5 **Blogroll.** A list of links to other blogs, which are in the same topic area as yours, or which you think your readers will also be interested in. These links between blogs can help drive traffic to them, particularly in a niche field.

6 **RSS feed.** RSS stands for 'Really Simple Syndication', and is just a technical way of saying 'subscription'. It means people can click on a special link to receive your latest posts as soon as they are published. There are a number of ways they can receive these – in an RSS reader, on a personalised home page – even by email. You don't need to worry about how it works, as it's a standard feature that comes with your blog. There are, however, things you can do to manage and promote your feed, which we will look at later in this chapter.

Crucially, a blog is a conversation – not a lecture. Don't just use a blog as a press-release delivery mechanism. It is far more than that. It is a way for you to start a discussion, provide useful information, and connect with your community.

Why blogging works for business

Blogs are no longer just personal diaries. The business case for blogging is compelling. With a blog you can:

1 **Build trust** with your potential customers and clients. Today, trust is in 'people like me' rather than in large organisations. We choose to do business with people we know, like and trust. Your blog is an important way for people to get to know you.

2 **Build an audience.** One reason to start a blog – even before your business is properly up and running – is to start building an audience. Once you have a niche community following, you will be able to find a way to monetise them later – by selling them products and services that fit with their interests.

3 **Increase search engine visibility.** Google and other search engines love blogs. This is because of the way search engine algorithms work. Google believes a site is more valuable if it has regularly updated content – which a well-maintained blog has. It also prefers sites that other people link to – and people are more likely to link to specific blog posts than a static, brochure-style website. By writing about topical issues on your blog – such as the latest developments in your field or a conference you recently attended – you will be more findable because you will be writing about things people are more likely to be searching for. And finally, the more blog posts you write, the more pages you create for Google to index. These things combine to improve your natural search engine rankings.

4 **Drive traffic to your business website.** The search engine friendliness of blogs, combined with other ways you can market your blog, plus regularly updated, quality, topical content, will keep traffic coming to your blog. Ideally, your blog will be on the same domain as your business website and integrated with it – or at least have a prominent link to your business website.

5 **Position yourself as an expert in your field.** By writing insightful, quality posts, and providing useful information to your community, you can become seen as an expert in your niche – whether that is tax law, flower arranging, or coarse fishing.

6 **Reach a wider market.** More people can find you in more ways if you have a blog.

7 **Create value** for your clients or customers by providing useful content.

8 **Learn from your customers** by inviting comments and feedback from them. A blog can be useful for doing ad hoc bits of market research, and helps to keep you closer to your market so that you're more aware of what they want.

9 **Create networking opportunities** you never knew existed. It's not just clients and customers who will find you via your blog but also potential business partners. And if you successfully position yourself as an expert, you may even find that speaking, consulting and writing opportunities come your way.

---

blogging in action

Stormhoek Wines (www.stormhoek.com)

Stormhoek Wines (www.stormhoek.com) is a small South African winery. They went from being a 50,000 case winery in 2005 to 280,000 cases in 2007 using a budget of less than £20,000 – and the power of blogging.

They started a blog in 2005 – though that wasn't their main strategy. They really wanted to engage with other bloggers, and having their own blog was a route to doing that. They used 'blogger outreach' as their main strategy, and offered a free bottle of wine to bloggers. They had certain criteria, such as targeting technology blogs, and blogs that were at least six months old. But the free wine got them talked about in the blogosphere, which pushed up their natural search engine rankings, made them more visible, and gave their sales reps a nice story to tell to wine merchants. It also increased sales.

They sent about 100 bottles to UK bloggers, 50 to Ireland and a few to France, with no requirement to write positively about it – or indeed to write anything. But the bloggers did, motivated by a desire to write about an interesting 'web 2.0' marketing experiment. They took the wine to geek dinners. They put pictures on Flickr. Word spread. It became the geek wine of choice. It became the Microsoft house wine. Stormhoek was the unofficial cult wine of Silicone Valley – despite being made 7,000 miles away instead of 30 miles down the road in Napa Valley. The campaign made the *Advertising Age* Marketing 50.

Hugh McLeod (http://gapingvoid.com), the ad-man turned professional blogger behind the campaign, describes the wine as a 'social object' – something that may be digital, intellectual or physical, around which people gather to talk about. Hugh would go so far as to say we're not in the business of creating products any more – we're in the business of creating social objects.

> Since then, their blog has become their main business website, and includes
> prominent links to their social media presence on other sites: Facebook, Flickr and
> YouTube.
> **Get the idea**: You don't always have to start your own blog to benefit from the
> blogosphere. Do you have something you can give away? Find bloggers in your
> topic area using http://blogsearch.google.com, and target the ones with a
> larger readership for a giveaway; or invite them to run a competition with their
> readers, with your product as the prize.

Get up to speed with blogging

First of all, familiarise yourself with the blogosphere by reading a few blogs
to get the hang of the conventions, possibilities and styles. Search for blogs
in your field at www.technorati.com or http://blogsearch.google.com. Subscribe
to a few RSS feeds to get the hang of how these work. The blogs you discover at this stage will be useful later when you come to put together your
blogroll, and when you're looking for topics to write about.

Then take the plunge! Here are the steps you need to take to get your
blog up and running – and other people reading it:

1 Choose a blogging strategy.

2 Create your blog.

3 Set up your RSS feed.

4 Write your first post.

Choose a blogging strategy

In order to get the most from blogging, it pays to spend a bit of time
thinking about what you want to achieve. There is more than one way to
benefit from the power of the blogosphere – and not all of them involve
starting your own blog. You can, of course, use these in combination:

1 **Start your own blog**. This is the obvious strategy. But if you're not
   quite ready to jump into the blogosphere, but want to benefit from
   the power of blogging, try the following. These can also be used – and
   become more effective – when you have your own blog.

2   **Comment on other blogs.** Often overlooked, but an important way
    of raising your profile. If you read those related blogs you found,
    particularly those with a large readership, and make a considered,
    thoughtful comment on someone else's post, you've just contributed to
    a conversation and produced some useful content. Your comment will
    link back to your own blog or website, and drive traffic to it. Do write
    something useful and interesting that contributes to the discussion,
    though – don't just try to sell something or say 'visit my site'. You
    probably won't get past the moderation controls – and it's just rude.

3   **Go on a blog tour.** This goes one step further than comments, as
    it involves writing actual posts on other people's blogs. Approach
    owners of blogs in your field, and ask if you can write a guest posting.
    Pitch an idea or topic. If you write a post that is interesting and useful
    to that blog's readership, the blog owner is quite likely to welcome
    your contribution (it cuts down on his or her workload), and you
    benefit from exposure to a new audience and a link back to your own
    blog or website. The concept of a 'blog tour' refers to a planned series
    of such guest postings on different blogs, usually over a limited time
    period leading up to a product launch, or to raise awareness of a new
    business, service or website.

4   **Blogger outreach.** The approach Stormhoek Wines used. Possibly
    the least used approach, but can be an effective way to engage the
    blogosphere and get other people talking about your stuff, especially
    if you have a free sample you can give away.

Create your blog

Once you have a blog set up, it is incredibly easy to manage and maintain. The only technical bit is installing the platform in the first place,
and this is the part you may need some help with if you're not a
tech-head. There are a range of platform options, including Blogger,
WordPress, Typepad and Movable Type. I always recommend WordPress
to my clients, and use it on all my own blogs: it's free, robust, and end-
lessly customisable with 'themes' (designs), 'plugins' and 'widgets'
(which add extra functionality). Whichever platform you choose, your
blogging options really boil down to two choices:

1   **Hosted externally.** If you use www.blogger.com or http://wordpress.com,
    you can be up and running in a few minutes. You don't have to
    worry about installing software, buying web space, or owning a

domain name. This is the easy option, and worth considering if you just want to try out blogging to see if it's for you, or if you don't yet have a website or domain name. The downside is that it looks less professional, and you're stuck with a domain name that has blogspot or wordpress in it, such as http://yourname.blogspot.com or http://yourname.wordpress.com.

2 **Hosted on your own server.** If you own some web space and have your own domain name (see Chapter 3), you can go to http://wordpress.org, download the latest copy of WordPress for free, and install it on your server. This not only looks more professional, but also means:

- your blog stays on your own business website – essential for driving web traffic to your business

- your blog is customisable with a wide range of free or commercially available themes

- you can go a stage further if you wish, and create a bespoke theme – or have one created for you – so that your blog matches your business site, or simply looks exactly as you want

- you have access to a vast number of plugins and widgets to extend the functionality of your blog.

If you start off with wordpress.com, you can always move to a wordpress.org blog later. It is even possible to migrate your content across from wordpress.com to wordpress.org.

The technicalities of WordPress installation are beyond the scope of this book. Some Internet service providers (ISPs) allow a one-click install of WordPress from your control panel, which saves the bother of installing it yourself. If you download the software from http://wordpress.org, you will need to ensure your server has access to the latest version of the programming language PHP, and that you can connect the software to a MySQL database. If in doubt, ask your ISP.

You will also need to decide if you want the software installed in your 'root' directory, e.g. www.mybusiness.com, or in a sub-directory such as www.mybusiness.com/blog. There is a view that you should always install it in the root to make your content easier for search engines to find – but I don't think this makes a lot of difference. What works less well is if you have your blog as a stand-alone site, apart from your business site,

❝ what works less well is if you have your blog as a stand-alone site on a separate domain ❞

on a separate domain, such as http://mybusiness.wordpress.com or http://mybusiness.blogspot.com (blogs hosted on wordpress.com or Blogger), or www.myblog.com (a completely different domain name). Although you might get a lot of traffic to your blog, you're not driving traffic to your business website. There are ways around this, such as prominent links to your business site, and compelling reasons to visit it, such as special offers for blog readers – but it's more powerful to keep it all integrated on the same domain.

Think about whether your business blog is to be a discrete section of your website, or if you want your entire website to be a blog. There are advantages to the latter – the main one being that you can also use WordPress as a content management system. This means that, in addition to adding and updating blog posts through a simple web-based interface, you can also add or update pages. All the pages on your website, yourself, without needing any technical knowledge.

Widgets and plugins

WordPress widgets and plugins are additional bits of software that add extra functionality to your blog. They are usually free, and are incredibly useful. Widgets usually appear in your sidebar, and include functions such as your blogroll, a list of your blog authors, your latest tweets, or an RSS feed from another blog.

Widgets are for everyone, but plugins are only available to you if you use http://wordpress.org – the version that you download and host yourself – rather than http://wordpress.com – the version that they host for you. You can find a comprehensive directory of plugins at http://wordpress.org/extend/plugins. Some of the ones I find useful include:

Contact Form (http://wordpress.org/extend/plugins/contact-form-7) – there are plenty of plugins out there that will enable you to include a simple contact form to a page on your blog. An easy way for people to get in touch with you.

flickrRSS (http://eightface.com/wordpress/flickrrss/) – displays your Flickr photos on your blog.

Sexy Bookmarks (http://wordpress.org/extend/plugins/sexybookmarks) – will add social bookmarking buttons such as 'Tweet this' to your blog posts. See Chapter 15 for more information.

WordPress Audio Player (http://wpaudioplayer.com/) – with this plugin installed, the link to any MP3 file you include in a post or page will become a Flash media player, so that visitors can play an audio file directly from your blog. This is essential if you are delivering a podcast via your blog (see Chapter 7).

WP-Cumulus (http://www.roytanck.com/2008/03/15/wp-cumulus-released/) – there are many plugins to display a 'tag cloud' on your blog – a collection of your keyword tags with the more frequently used tags appearing larger. WP-Cumulus gives you a great, animated version, with your tags spinning in a 3-D globe.

WP Status Notifier (http://wordpresssupplies.com/wordpress-plugins/status-notifier/) – a simple yet essential plugin if you run a multi-author blog, such as a business blog where a number of your colleagues contribute posts. It simply sends you (or another blog administrator) an email whenever a contributed post is pending your review and approval before it is published. Something you wouldn't otherwise know without this handy plugin.

Set up your RSS feed

One of the things that makes a blog a blog rather than an ordinary, static website is that your readers can subscribe to your latest postings. They do this through your RSS feed. This stands for Really Simple Syndication, and is a standard feature that comes with your blogging software. By clicking on an RSS icon on your blog or in the web address bar, your readers will be taken to a page where they can opt to subscribe in which-ever way suits them – say, by adding your feed to their favourite RSS newsreader, or to their personalised Google home page.

Why do you want people to subscribe to your RSS feed? Because it means they don't have to keep checking back to your blog to see whether or not you've posted anything new. This is especially important if you don't post very often! If people are subscribed to your feed, they will be alerted, in a way that suits them, whenever you post something new.

This comes with your blog and works automatically – you don't need to do anything. But you will have many more options if you sign up – for free – to www.feedburner.com. Not only do you get access to statistics about how many people subscribe to your feed, which posts are most popular and clicked on but you also get a wealth of ways to promote your feed.

These include a counter to put on your blog, showing the number of your subscribers; some code to add to your blog to encourage people to subscribe at the end of every post; and, most usefully, an email delivery option (see Chapter 5).

quick win

Find topics to write about

You have your blog set up. Now, what are you going to write about? If you are a business-to-business (B2B) company, write about developments in the industry you serve. If you are business-to-consumer (B2C) company, what do your customers care about? You can write about your latest company news, products and services – but it's best not to do this too often. Resist the urge to use your blog as a press-release delivery mechanism, since that won't do a lot for your traffic. Rather than a hard sell, focus instead on useful information that your community will value, and on what your target audience wants to read about.

Include plenty of keywords relating to your business, and focus each blog posting on one topic. This will help your search engine rankings. Follow the journalistic principle of starting with the headline, getting the main story into your opening line and then get more detailed.

To find inspiration for topics to write about, do the following:

■ **Read other blogs** and subscribe to the RSS feeds of ones that are relevant to you and your readers.

■ **Use Google Alerts** (www.google.com/alerts) for email updates in your area of interest.

■ **Carry a notebook** to jot down ideas as they occur to you.

■ **Be topical**. If you write about, say, the latest Budget statement, or an industry awards dinner you attended, chances are people will be searching for information on that subject.

■ **Solve a problem** for your readers. Any blog post that starts with the words 'How to...' is usually popular.

■ **Create a list**. Blog posts that start '10 ways to...' or '6 essential resources for...' are also popular.

Write your first post

WordPress comes with a powerful built-in text editor. Use it to create new blog posts and pages.

figure 6.1 Write your first post

1 Add a title for your blog post. Be aware that this also appears in the permalink (the URL for the individual blog post), so will be the first thing search engines see. Make it relevant to your post and think about keywords.

2 Type your post directly into the text window. If you want to copy and paste from a Word document, you will need to strip out the hidden formatting tags that Word puts into documents, since these will affect the look and format of your post on the blog. To do this, simply click on the **HTML** tab, paste in your text, then switch back to the **Visual** tab to continue editing. You can also use the HTML tab to enter HTML into your post.

3 To enter a link, highlight text you want to turn into a link, and click the chain icon. Enter the full URL of the page you want to link to, and a title for the link (optional – this displays when someone hovers over the link). Click update.

4 To enter an image, click the 'Add an image' button next to the Upload/Insert menu just above the text editing window. You can also use the icons here to upload video, audio or other media.

5 To add a video from YouTube, simply copy and paste the embed code supplied by YouTube for the video you want into the HTML window.

6 When you have finished creating your post, add it to a Category. The default category for blog posts is 'Uncategorized'. By putting your blog posts into meaningful categories (you can choose more than one for a single post), you create another way for people to navigate to the content they want.

7 Add tags – keywords that describe what your blog post is about – to further help people to find your post.

8 Once you've finished, you can save your post as a Draft, Preview how it will look before publishing, or hit the Publish button to publish it now. If you want to publish it at some point in the future, just amend the publication date settings. This is useful if you want to write several posts at once, and release them over time – perhaps while you are away.

Manage the workload

In 2008, the New York Times identified a phenomenon called 'death by blogging'[3] – exhausted bloggers in digital sweat-shops trying to keep up with the constant demand of the always-on Internet economy for fresh news, insight and comment. Some people will tell you that you need to update a blog daily for it to be of any value. How on earth can you keep up?

Stop. Take a deep breath. Relax. It doesn't have to be that way. First of all, you don't need to blog every day. Yes, you need to maintain the freshness of your content to keep people coming back, **you don't need to blog every day** and keep the benefit of those search engine results. But if you neglect your blog for a few days – even a few weeks – it's not a disaster. Blogging is a bit like gardening. You do need to water your plants regularly – but you can leave them a while before they start dying. It's also authentic to blog when you have something to say, rather than to force yourself to write something – anything – just to fill space.

3 www.nytimes.com/2008/04/06/technology/06sweat.html

That said, those plants – and your blog traffic – will eventually wither and die. So how will you find the time to keep your blog up to date?

1 **Schedule time for blogging.** Easier said than done, but you should set aside some time for updating your blog as you would for any other marketing activity – either daily or weekly, depending on how often you plan to write.

2 **Batch process your posts.** Write a number of posts in one go, and then schedule them to appear over the next several days or weeks. With WordPress, you can set blog posts to publish on a specific date and time in the future.

3 **Write short posts.** You don't have to write a 2,000 word essay all the time. Break up long posts into chunks and publish them over several days. People prefer to read material on the Web in bite-sized chunks. You might consider writing one longer post, such as a feature or 'think piece' once a month – and write shorter posts the rest of the time.

4 **Re-blog other people's posts.** Scan the latest blog posts in your topic using your RSS reader, or cast an eye over your Twitter friends to find interesting relevant blog posts. You don't always have to write original material yourself. You can highlight an extract from someone else's blog – making sure you credit the author and link to the full post, of course. You may want to add some words of your own, providing your take on the subject, and contextualising it for your readers. This is more useful than just posting links to other blogs.

5 **Save time with Zemanta.** As well as allowing readers to re-blog extracts from the front end, a plugin called Zemanta (www.zemanta.com) gives you a bit of editorial help in the back end. As you write, it will automatically suggest links, images and related blog posts that you can add to your post with a single click.

6 **Dictate your posts.** If you really want to speed things up, why not invest in some dictation software? Mac Speech Dictate is excellent for the Mac; or try Dragon NaturallySpeaking for the PC. Bloggers tend to have a conversational style, after all.

7 **Don't do it all yourself.** Invite other people in your business to write blog postings. This shares the workload and involves and engages them. You may want to invite external people to do an occasional guest blog spot. Multi-author blogs are easy to manage with WordPress. You can even outsource your blogging and have someone ghost-write posts for you. Check out www.elance.com as a

starting point. Is this authentic? It's a debatable point. I've never done it – though I know respected bloggers who have, and I wouldn't rule it out. I think that, so long as you see and edit these posts before you publish them, and ideally put them in your own voice, it's no less authentic than a newspaper editor commissioning an editorial. You will have, after all, briefed on the topic – the research and writing just happens to have been done by a freelancer. You're still providing valuable content to your readership, in the niche topic area you have identified. And it's better than blogging yourself to death or neglecting your blog for months because you're too busy.

Measure your results

1 **Web stats.** Look at your website analytics package, such as Google Analytics or Clicky, to analyse how much traffic you're getting and from where. Spot which are the most popular posts, and write more of them.

2 **Feed stats.** Look at your statistics in www.feedburner.com, for a breakdown of who is accessing your RSS feed and how. You may want to include a counter of subscribers on your blog – if your numbers are impressive enough.

3 **Rankings.** Look at where you site ranks by topic on www.technorati.com.

4 **Conversational index.** We started this chapter by describing markets as conversations, and blogs as conversation starters. Well, you can measure the level of conversational engagement your blog has. Your conversational index is the number of blog comments divided by the number of blog posts. You're aiming for a number above 1 with this one. WordPress will display a count of these in your back-end dashboard. If you're so minded, you could even use this measure over a discrete time period, or for a specific category.

Take action

- **Subscribe** to a few blogs in your area to familiarise yourself with the blogosphere. Find these using http://blogsearch.google.com.

- **Create** your blog using WordPress.

- **Manage** your RSS feed by signing up to www.feedburner.com.

- **Find** some topics to write about.

- **Write** your first post!

- **Market** your blog by pulling it into the Notes function in your Facebook page (see Chapter 11) and automatically tweeting your blog posts using www.twitterfeed.com (see Chapter 13).

Podcast for profit

How to attract an audience of loyal listeners

Podcasting is an intimate medium – like radio – and a way of building loyal relationships with your audience as well as conveying useful information and promoting your business without a hard sell. The barriers to producing both audio and video have plummeted in recent years. You no longer need expensive equipment to create these engaging forms of media, a licence to deliver them to your audience, or a vast audience to be profitable. Just a niche topic area, something useful to say, and a willingness to communicate.

What is a podcast?

The term 'podcast' was coined as recently as 2004, by John Ben Hammersley in the *Guardian* newspaper. It is a portmanteau of the words 'pod', from iPod, and 'broadcasting'. The word is a little misleading, however, since you don't need an iPod or any MP3 player to listen to podcasts: about half of those who listen to them do so from their computer. Despite the radio show format many adopt, it is also not broadcasting either – quite the opposite, in fact, since podcasts reach niche audiences rather than the mass market. The term 'narrowcasting' is more appropriate.

Another thing a podcast is not is a static audio file on a web page. The thing that turns audio files into podcasts is the ability to subscribe to new episodes as they are released, like a magazine. This is achieved by wrapping the audio files in an RSS feed. That sounds frighteningly technical – but isn't. It just means you deliver them on a blog.

When someone subscribes, using a service such as iTunes, new episodes are downloaded when they are ready, and can be listened to from your computer or portable MP3 player. This makes them 'time-shifted media' – unlike a radio show that you have to tune in to at a specific time, a podcast can be listened to whenever and wherever suits the listener. Shows may be regular, e.g. weekly – or you may choose to do a limited run of a few shows leading up to a product launch or event.

Podcasts can also be video files – sometimes called vodcasts. We will concentrate mainly on audio in this chapter, and there is more information on video production in the next chapter.

Podcasts are usually free, but it is also possible to charge for them. However, if you are using a podcast to market your business, it is best to keep it free, and not even charge the price of an email registration. You want to build an audience, not barriers.

Why podcasting works for business

Podcasts have the power to create a bond between you and your customers. Nothing engages your customers like audio and video. Speaking to people directly helps build trust, convey information and articulate what your business has to offer in a far more effective way than reading brochure text on a website.

❝ nothing engages your customers like audio and video ❞

A podcast is also another way for people to discover you, since people search on iTunes and other directories for podcasts in their area of interest. By connecting with this community of interest, you can generate customer loyalty – and new business.

Podcasting works for your business by creating a community around it, based on the usefulness of the information you share with potential clients and customers. This also positions you as an expert in your field, and someone who is committed enough to it to put on a show. It is important to use podcasting in this way, rather than as a sales pitch. This is not the place to sell your wares. If you want to do an audio ad, call your local radio station. A podcast, like other forms of social media, should focus on your audience and providing them with something of value. Include a call to action, and the sales will come later.

A podcast, like a blog, is a content tool that becomes more powerful the more content you add. A regular podcast, like a regular blog, builds up a back catalogue of information that people will keep discovering. And since each episode of your podcast will be delivered on a separate page of your blog, along with show notes and possibly even a transcript, there is plenty of textual content and links for search engines to index too.

podcasting in action

Wiggly Wigglers (www.wigglywigglers.co.uk)

Heather Gorringe runs a small organic gardening mail order company called Wiggly Wigglers from her farm in Herefordshire. They sell things like wormeries, live mealworms and bird seed. In 2005, they abandoned traditional marketing in favour of a blog, an email newsletter and a weekly half-hour podcast that attracts thousands of listeners around the world. They have since also taken advantage of Facebook, YouTube and Twitter. The shift to online marketing saw their marketing costs plummet to a fraction of their traditional marketing costs and increased their reach.

The podcast has been their most successful marketing tool, and has won them awards such as Best Gardening Podcast in 2007. The secret of its success is its niche subject matter shared with passion. Alongside Farmer Phil, Richard and Monty, Heather covers issues such as the environment, wildlife, gardening, farming and biodiversity with lots of personality and very little selling. While she does sometimes mention special offers and latest products, the focus is much more on communicating organic gardening tips, and banter with her colleagues – information her community of interest find useful, and an informal style they connect with. It leads people back on to the website, which she mentions on the podcast.

The show has a lot of fans, and she includes them in the show, regularly playing in voicemails from listeners and reading out emails. There's a real sense of community that has built up around her business, which would never have been possible with a magazine advert. Heather had tried magazine adverts during their traditional marketing years, but ads cost a fortune, and are only there once, in one issue. With a podcast, you're up there forever. People still discover her through podcasts she did years ago. She reaches a huge global audience and has been featured in foreign press such as the *San Francisco Chronicle*.

Thanks to their online marketing efforts, delivered in an authentic, engaging style, Wiggly Wigglers have not only built a successful business on a budget but also won awards, including recognition by Dell as the number one small business in the UK in their 2008 Small Business Excellence Awards.

> ▶ **Get the idea**: You don't need a qualification in radio production or a recording studio to make great, engaging audio. Convey your passion, learn as you go along and involve your audience. Use your podcast to communicate useful information, rather than sales messages. Build community, and the sales will come later.

Get up to speed with podcasting

Podcasting can seem an intimidating social media tool to use, as there is more to it than starting a Facebook group or setting up a blog. But it is really not that scary if you approach it with the same principles as other forms of social media. Think about what valuable, useful content you can provide. Focus on your audience, be relevant, authentic and informal and include a call to action at the end. Don't go for a hard sell – think infotainment rather than infomercial, and leave them wanting more.

The technical aspects are also fairly straightforward if you follow these steps: plan, record, produce, deliver and promote.

1 Plan your podcast – choose a style and format.
2 Record your podcast – choose your equipment.
3 Produce your podcast – editing, post-production and music.
4 Deliver your podcast via your blog.
5 Promote your podcast – get listed in iTunes.

Plan your podcast

What sort of podcast are you going to produce? What works well in your market? Start with a search in iTunes for keywords in your field, and see what podcasts are available. Subscribe to those that interest you. iTunes has a dedicated section for video podcasts too – have a look there if you're considering video podcasting.

Audio or video?

One of your first decisions is whether to produce an audio or video podcast. This might partly be constrained by budget available, since audio podcasts are generally cheaper to produce. But they also work well for communicating knowledge. If your content is primarily interviews, you may as well do an audio podcast rather than a video with talking heads. Video podcasts work well when there is a practical, visual element to what you want to communicate. If your content is based on tutorials, you can also produce a video podcast cheaply by using some software called Camtasia to record PowerPoint slides, or whatever you're doing on-screen, for example to illustrate how to use software or web services. The video tutorials for this book are an example of that.

Choosing a style and format

For a video podcast based on online tutorials it's fine to do the voiceover yourself, but for an audio podcast it is more interesting for the listener to have a co-host than just to talk at people yourself. Interviewing guests also breaks things up and adds new voices.

Have a listen to some podcasts in your area, or just those whose style you like. You don't have to copy your competition, but if you find a style you like, feel free to adapt it for your niche. Do you want to do a magazine-style show with co-hosts and interviews like the Guardian Media Talk podcast, for example? Listening carefully to well-produced shows like this will give you some clues as to where to play in the intro music, and ideas like highlighting forthcoming interviews with some extracts at the top of the show.

❝ have a listen to some podcasts in your area ❞

How long should your podcast be? The received wisdom, based on various surveys, has tended to be an absolute maximum of 20–30 minutes for an audio podcast and 5 minutes for a video podcast. Shorter is generally better with podcasting, however – people have short attention spans online, and even 3–5 minutes for an audio podcast may be sufficient. However, this isn't right for every audience. Invite feedback on your first few episodes, and your audience will soon tell you if they think it's too long or too short.

Once you start podcasting, don't feel you have to stay on a treadmill of producing half an hour every week forever. You can also do a limited-run podcast of, say, four to eight episodes leading up to a launch or event; or do your podcasts in seasons of six episodes at a time. Survey your audience to find out what works for them – but also plan your podcasting to fit realistically with the demands of your business.

Podcasting styles include round-table discussions, a single interview each episode, and a magazine-style programme with several segments that are common to every show. Plan your format as you might for a radio or TV programme. For example:

Intro	Industry news	Feature/ Interview	Tips/How-to feature	Ending

Then sketch out a grid to plan your shows in advance. You can record some items in advance – just keep a note on your grid of which things are yet to be recorded. Think about your timings at this stage too. For example:

Item	Duration	Ep1	Ep2	Ep3
Intro	00:30	Intro	Intro	Intro
News	04:30	Item name	Item name	Item name
Interview	06:00	Item name	Item name	Item name
Tips	03:30	Item name	Item name	Item name
Ending	00:30	Music	Music	Music
TOTAL	15:00			
			Recorded	To be recorded

Record your podcast

You don't need to hire a recording studio to capture good-quality audio. The quality of your microphones is the most important factor.

Hardware

Clip-on tie microphones offer good quality, especially for round-table discussions. For recording yourself directly on to your computer, use a microphone that plugs into your computer's USB port rather than one with a standard jack – the quality is much better. You can pick up a good USB microphone, such as the Samson C01U USB Studio Condenser Microphone, for about $100/£75.

The M-Audio Microtrack 24/96 or Zoom H2 Handy Recorder (both about $200/£150) are used by many podcasters – useful for recording interviews on the move.

Interviews

Interviews are a great way of providing useful information and new perspectives to your listeners. You can do interviews in person or using free Internet telephony such as Skype (www.skype.com) with a recording application called Pamela (www.pamela-systems.com).

Give your guests a fighting chance by giving them some idea of what you want to ask them first – a list of questions or topics in advance. That doesn't mean that you should script your podcast, or that you can't explore other questions and topics that arise during the conversation – it just primes your guest on what to expect, and helps them prepare their thoughts. It will produce a more useful interview from a more confident guest.

It's usually a good idea to have your guests sign an interview release. You can do this electronically using a WordPress plugin that you can find at http://mwgblog.com/archives/2007/01/01/podcast-release-wordpress-plugin. Bear in mind general journalistic guidelines and ethics when interviewing. See the UK Press Complaints Commission's 'Editors' Code of Practice' at www.pcc.org.uk/cop/practice.html for an example of this. Above all, don't record anyone without their permission.

Produce your podcast

Once you have recorded your audio content, in the form of interviews and discussion, it's time for post-production. This means editing out pauses and mistakes (don't over edit, though), piecing together your different items and interviews, adding any music and sound effects, and exporting the whole thing as an MP3 file.

Audio editing software

To edit your audio, use some great free software called Audacity for the PC or Mac (http://audacity.sourceforge.net). Mac users can also use Garageband (www.apple.com/ilife/garageband). Audacity is very powerful and can be used to work on multiple, overlapping tracks on a single timeline – such as your introduction, interviews and music – and then combine them into a single file. See the website at www.getuptospeed.biz/audacity for video tutorials on getting started with Audacity.

Music

You can't just include any music from your CD collection – that's illegal! Make sure you have permission to use any music you need. Music Alley (www.musicalley.com – formerly the Podsafe Music Network) is a good place to find licensed music. However, for an opening theme tune, I recommend AKM Music (www.akmmusic.co.uk) – a great source of affordable, licensed music used by big brands and broadcasters such as the BBC. With a large database of music categorised by style, you're sure to find something appropriate that fits your 'audio branding'. For free sound effects, try Soundsnap (www.soundsnap.com).

> 66 make sure you have permission to use any music you need 55

Output

Output your finished work as an MP3 file. You can do this with Audacity, but you will need to install something called a LAME MP3 Encoder first. This is free, and instructions are supplied by Audacity. Be sure to add ID3 tags to your MP3 file too – these specify information that is contained within your audio file such as genre, author and title. Do a search for 'ID3 tag editor' to find free software you can use to do this.

Deliver your podcast

Host your audio files

Now that you've created your MP3 audio file, it's time to share it with the world! The first step is to host it on a website. You have two options here:

1 A podcast hosting service – there are various services that will host your audio or video podcast for you, such as www.libsyn.com and www.hipcast.com. These will also provide statistics, including number of downloads.

2 Your regular web hosting service – just upload your audio files to your normal web server in a separate folder called 'podcasts'. You will be able to access statistics from your web-stats package.

Whichever option you choose, you will have access to more detailed information on your subscribers via your Feedburner account.

Create a blog or a blog category

Next, you need to deliver your audio files on a blog. Create a new blog post for each podcast episode, either on a blog dedicated to your podcast, or on your business blog with a 'podcast' category. Include a title, and show notes. These should comprise a short paragraph explaining what is on the episode, a list of topics or items covered with timings, and links to any websites mentioned.

Don't forget to create a link to the MP3 audio file you uploaded, and make sure it can be played on the page. Use a blog theme or WordPress plugin (such as WordPress Audio Player – http://wpaudioplayer.com) that automatically turns links to audio files into a media player, so that people can listen to your podcast directly from your website without having to download it first.

Create an RSS feed in Feedburner

Whether your podcast is delivered on a dedicated blog or a discrete category of your main blog, an RSS feed will be created for it. However, don't use this as the main feed for your podcast, such as the one you submit to iTunes. Create a new feed in Feedburner first.

❝ make sure you check the 'I am a podcaster' box ❞

This is as simple as it is to create a Feedburner feed for your blog – just make sure you check the 'I am a podcaster' box when you set up your feed in order to access the additional options you need for a podcast feed.

Select the 'include iTunes podcasting elements' in Feedburner and add the data iTunes requires there. Additional items you need to include in your RSS feed, to provide the data that iTunes and other directories require, include a category, subcategory, description and keywords for your podcast. You also need a 'podcover' – a 300 × 300 pixel .jpg graphic that is the equivalent to a record sleeve or book jacket for your podcast. Enter a weblink for this in the image field.

If you use the PodPress plugin in WordPress, this data will already be included in your feed, and you won't need to enter it into Feedburner.

Feedburner will provide you with the same range of statistics and promotional tools, including subscription by email, as you get for a standard blog feed.

quick win

Create an instant podcast with AudioBoo (http://audioboo.fm)

AudioBoo launched in 2009, and is best thought of as 'audio Twitter'. It is a very easy way to create short audio files (up to 5 minutes long) from your iPhone or computer, and share them with your community. You can automatically tweet your 'boos' and share them on Facebook. What's more, people can subscribe to your boos in iTunes, making it an easy way to create an instant, ad hoc podcast without worrying about blogs, RSS feeds or recording equipment.

■ Create an account at http://audioboo.fm.

■ Upload a profile image, add a brief biography, and make sure to include your web address.

■ Before you start booing, do a keyword search to find some boos in your area of interest, to get a feel for what people are doing, and relevant people to follow.

■ If you have an iPhone, download the free iPhone app. It is also possible to record boos and upload them from your computer. But booing works best on the move.

■ Record your first boo. This doesn't have to be an interview – you can just introduce yourself and your new AudioBoo account and say what you'll be using it for. It doesn't have to be slick or professional. The beauty of AudioBoo is its brevity and immediacy.

■ Upload your boo along with a photo, which you can take with your iPhone if you are using the app. This might be of the person you were speaking to. Include a title for your boo, and tag it with some keywords to help people find it.

■ AudioBoo then creates a page for your boo, with a media player to play back your audio, the photo you uploaded, and a map showing where you recorded it – since your iPhone knows where you are! You can opt out of the map if you want, and photos are optional too – but both add useful context.

■ Your page also includes social bookmarking buttons ('Tweet this', 'share on Facebook'), and a link to some embed code so that other people can embed your audio on their own blog or web page. You can also use this on your own site to raise awareness of your boos; and be sure to include a link on your website. Your AudioBoo profile page also includes buttons to subscribe to all of your boos by RSS or via iTunes.

■ Gain greater exposure for your boos by automatically tweeting them to your Twitter account. You can also automatically post them to Facebook, Posterous, FriendFeed and Tumblr. This has the added benefit of contributing useful content to those accounts.

■ Use AudioBoo whenever you have the chance to speak with an expert in your field at a conference or trade fair. Many people use AudioBoo to have a quick chat with conference speakers during breaks, drinks, or when they visit an exhibition stand. You may also want to share the logins with any colleagues who have an iPhone.

Promote your podcast

Get listed in iTunes

&& iTunes is the Google of podcast directories ""

iTunes is the Google of podcast directories – you absolutely must get it listed here. Others include PodBean.com, Podcast Alley, PodcastDirectory.com, Podcast Pickle, blubrry and Odeo – but the vast majority of people will go straight to iTunes.

1   Open the iTunes program. You can download this for free from www.apple.com/itunes if you don't have it.

2   Sign in to the iTunes Store. You'll need to create an account if you don't already have one.

3   Click on the 'Podcasts' section in the top navigation.

4   Click 'Submit a Podcast' in the right-hand menu.

5   Enter in your podcast feed URL. Make sure this is the one you created in Feedburner rather than your original feed address from your blog, so that Feedburner can track your stats.

6   Confirm the on-screen details, and click 'Submit'. You'll receive an email once your podcast has been accepted by iTunes. This typically takes about a week.

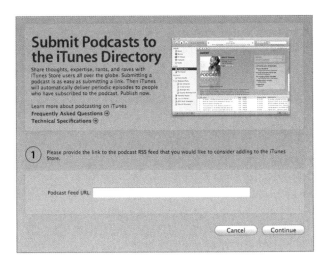

figure 7.1 Submit your podcast to iTunes

Promote your podcast online

Include a prominent link to your podcast on your own website, including buttons to subscribe in iTunes and by RSS. You might also consider a media player in your sidebar that plays your latest episode.

Make sure your show notes for each episode include plenty of keywords, and links to any websites you mention. You might even consider including a full transcript for each episode. This has two benefits: it makes your podcast more accessible; and it creates a large amount of text on your blog that can be indexed by search engines, making you more findable.

Every time you release a new episode, tell your email list, tweet about it, mention it on Facebook, LinkedIn or whichever social networks you use.

Create community

Just as people can leave text comments on your blog, invite them to submit audio comments on your podcast. Set up a Skype answering service, or use a blog plugin such as http://riffly.com to create a widget that captures audio or video comments. Not everyone is comfortable 'phoning in' comments, so invite comments by email, Twitter, Facebook, etc., or by commenting on the blog post for your podcast episode. You might even put a call out on Twitter for people to record their own AudioBoos for potential inclusion on your next podcast. Ask them to let you know when they've done this, or to add a hashtag specific to your podcast so you can find their comments. Make sure that people are clear about how their comments will be used.

Encourage your community to review your podcast on iTunes. A podcast with reviews is more likely to be subscribed to by new listeners.

Get interviewed on other podcasts

This is the podcasting equivalent of a guest posting on someone else's blog. Search iTunes for relevant podcasts, then approach the host by email.

Measure your success

Your customer ratings and reviews on iTunes will give you a sense of how well received your podcast is, along with feedback on your blog and audio comments. But there are other quantitative statistics you can use too:

◼ Your Feedburner statistics will tell you how many subscribers you have.

◼ Your web stats will tell you how many times your audio files have been downloaded.

◼ If you use a podcast hosting service, it will provide these stats.

◼ If you use unique landing pages – a web address that is only mentioned once on a specific podcast – you can measure how many people have taken action as a result of listening to your show and visited your website.

Take action

◼ **Listen** to a few podcasts in your field, to research your market.

◼ **Plan** your podcast style and format.

◼ **Record** your first podcast – interview an expert in your field.

◼ **Produce** your first podcast – familiarise yourself with Audacity.

◼ **Deliver** your podcast using a blog and Feedburner.

◼ **List** your podcast in iTunes.

◼ **Promote** your podcast on your website, with email and via your social networks.

8

Lights, camera, action!

How to produce online video on a budget

The wide take-up of broadband has made watching video online an integral part of many people's Internet browsing experience. It is now possible to watch entire feature films and TV shows online – something unthinkable just a few years ago. You no longer need a vast budget and a film crew to produce compelling video. The barriers to entry to using this medium have dropped significantly, and it is easier and cheaper than ever to create your own video and upload it to free video-sharing sites such as YouTube. As a business, you can use this as a powerful means of communicating directly with your clients and customers.

What is online video?

In October 2009, just five years after its launch, YouTube announced that it had reached the milestone of 1 billion views per day. It is by far the most popular video-sharing website according to Alexa. Other video-sharing sites are available, including blip.tv, 12seconds.tv, www.vimeo.com and sites aimed at Twitter users such as www.twitvid.com, but the sheer size and reach of YouTube makes this an important place to be if you want to engage your customers with video.

❝ the sheer size and reach of YouTube makes this an important place to be ❞

While putting a static piece of video on your website will engage your visitors and help your search engine results, it is not social media. If you upload your video to a video-sharing site and then embed it back on your site (simple to do with the code supplied), it provides another way for people to find and interact with you. They can comment on your video, add it to their 'favourites' and even embed it in their own websites or blogs.

Why online video works for business

Video works because it offers you a chance to show your wares to prospective customers or clients – whether you're a plumber, a hypnotherapist or a travel agent. It works particularly well where there is a visual element to your business – such as video tours of your properties if you are a real estate agent. But most businesses can find a way to use video successfully. In addition, video will:

- Boost your search engine rankings if you include it on your website. Search engines like websites with rich media content.
- Provide another way for people to find you. People search on YouTube as well as Google.
- Enhance your brand recognition.
- Encourage people to pass on your marketing message. If your video contains information of interest to a niche audience, bloggers writing about your subject area can embed your videos into their posts.
- Put a human face on your business.
- Educate your market, especially if your product or service is complicated to explain.
- Reduce the amount of time you spend on customer support and queries, by providing all the instruction your customers need in video tutorials. Useful if you sell software or other technical products, for example.
- Screen out the wrong type of client for your business. Sometimes, if people don't understand your product or service, you can waste time on a prospective client before either of you realise that what he or she needs and what you can offer don't match. Video is one of the clearest ways to articulate exactly what it is that you do.

online video in action

Will it Blend? (www.youtube.com/user/blendtec)

Since 2006 Blendtec have been filming their CEO, Tom Dickson, attempting to grind up various household objects and asking one simple question: Will it blend? Millions of people have watched the videos, on YouTube or their Will it Blend microsite at www.blendtec.com/willitblend, as objects as diverse as baseballs and cameras were lightheartedly yet efficiently destroyed by the Blendtec blender.

When Apple's iPad launched in April 2010 they, of course, blended it as almost seven million people watched in the two months after upload. They then ran a cheeky competition, in recognition of how opinion was divided on the new gadget: you could win a Blendtec blender plus either an intact iPad or the blended iPad remains. Competitions and giveaways are also promoted on their Facebook and Twitter pages, and their blog. Social media tools are more powerful when combined.

The videos are fun, communicate a key brand message ('the world's strongest blender'), and have generated headlines. But what about sales? Speaking in January 2009 – on YouTube, of course – Tom Dickson said: 'We're the 16th most subscribed to director on YouTube, and the 30th most watched. And our sales are up 700% since we started this Will It Blend campaign!'[4]

figure 8.1 Blendtec iPad giveaway video on YouTube

Source: www.youtube.com/watch?v=z_BshfWGQos

---

4 www.youtube.com/watch?v=u6t92m1gwTY

> **Get the idea**: You don't have to demonstrate your product in a bland, corporate, infomercial style. If you can find a way to showcase your product in a fun, irreverent, entertaining way, you will attract more viewers and encourage them to pass on your video. Use YouTube to promote competitions and giveaways that lead people back on to your site.

Get up to speed with online video

How you go about creating your video content depends on how ambitious you want to be, the production values you deem necessary, the time you have available, your level of technical skill and what sort of video you want to produce. You don't need a film school degree to get started with your own videos. For a small investment you can buy a cheap camera and upload clips direct to YouTube. In this section, we shall look at how to:

1 Decide what to produce.

2 Choose your equipment.

3 Film a studio-based interview.

4 Edit and output your video.

5 Share your video.

Decide what to produce

Whether you do it yourself or hire a video production company, the first step is to decide exactly what sort of video you want to produce. As with any form of social media marketing, the content you produce must be guided by what your community of interest will find of value. This can be quite specific and niche – in fact it's better if it is. You're not competing with the high-end TV ads of big brand advertising either. Often a talking head is just fine.

❝ the content you produce must be guided by what your community of interest will find of value ❞

Lord Reith's mission statement for the British Broadcasting Corporation in 1927 – to inform, educate and entertain – is a good guiding principle for producing video to support your business. You do, of course, have a fourth goal – to sell – but if you think 'infotainment' rather than 'sales pitch', your video will be more engaging, more widely viewed, and more likely to be passed on.

Consider your reasons for wanting to use video. What are your goals? They might include to generate sales, drive traffic to your website, raise brand awareness or reduce customer support costs. Here are some options to consider:

■ A **welcome message** on your website shows a human face behind the business.

■ **Client testimonials** are more engaging and convincing if presented as a compilation of short video interviews rather than a few lines of text.

■ **Interviews**, discussions or pieces to camera, filmed in 'studio' conditions with professional lighting present a professional image, and can convey useful information about your product, service, or topic.

■ **Commercials** may seem obvious, but they can be the least effective option. If you have an existing TV ad or promotional video, there's no harm in repurposing this for your online marketing. But TV ads rarely work well at the tiny screen size and limited resolution available to you on most video-sharing sites. Even though you can maximise the screen, most people don't, and you lose valuable detail. Better to have a single close-up of a talking head, or something that works equally well at 480 × 295 pixels.

■ **Infomercials** are more interesting than straight video ads. If you can get across some useful information that also mentions your product or service, it's much more likely to be viewed and shared.

■ **Product demonstrations** work when your product needs explanation or instructions, and can cut down on customer support time. Do you run a garden centre? How about a video showing us how to prune the roses you sell? You will find plenty of examples of exactly that on YouTube.

■ **Training videos** are a softer sell, yet by providing useful information in your area of expertise (but with the web address of your business at the end), they will draw people on to your site. You might also consider creating longer tutorials or online courses to sell. Joseph Clough is a hypnosis trainer who promotes his training and self-development titles with videos about hypnosis at www.youtube.com/user/josephcloughhypnosis. If you have an area of expertise, why not show us what you can do?

Choose your equipment

Most forms of online marketing are free. However, like podcasting, in order to create video content, you will need to spend a bit of cash. The good news is that you don't necessarily need to spend a fortune. The minimum hardware you will require is a video camera and a computer. You will also need some video editing software.

Camera

You don't need high-end professional gear. Many video podcasters use the Flip video camera, a hand-held camera with surprisingly good quality for its size. It is easy to use, highly portable, and great for filming ad hoc interviews when you're visiting clients or attending events, or for filming yourself doing a piece to camera. It has a pop-out USB connector to plug straight into your computer and upload your video to your YouTube account, and holds about two hours of video. The downside is that the audio from the built-in microphone will never be as good as a soundtrack recorded using external microphones. If you use the Flip, be sure to be quite close to your subject to get the best possible audio from it.

The Kodak Zi8 is a similarly priced alternative (both retail at around £150/$200), but comes with an external microphone jack, stores ten hours of video, and includes face tracking software. Both can record in HD.

You can even record and upload video from some smartphones, including the newer iPhones. This is useful for capturing current events – a growing trend as video and audio increasingly become part of the real-time web.

For something more substantial, you don't need a professional level video camera or something that will produce broadcast standard video (and, if you do, hire someone to do this for you). Go for a consumer video camera, but as high-end as you can afford. Key things to look out for include:

▪ The ability to attach external microphones. Don't rely on the built-in microphone on your camera. The end result may be too quiet, and sound a bit cheap. Use an external microphone, such as a shotgun microphone that is attached to the top of your camera. Better yet, record a separate soundtrack using the equipment discussed in the podcasting chapter. There's really nothing to beat clip-on tie microphones for quality of sound. You can record the sound direct on to your Microtrack or laptop, and use this in the final edit. If you do this, ensure you still record sound with the camera itself, since this will help you find your way around the filmed footage in the edit.

- Manual settings, such as the ability to set the 'white balance' and use manual focus.

- A camera that will record directly on to a digital hard drive, rather than on to mini discs, so that you don't have to waste time converting these into a format you can use.

- A camera that can record in 'high definition' isn't essential, but as video standards improve online, this could be useful.

Lights

If microphones are essential to the quality of your podcast, lighting is essential for video. If you're doing quick and informal clips, you may be able to get away with your Flip camera and use the available light. For something more professional, particularly for **❝ lighting is** studio-based interviews and pieces to camera, you **essential for video ❞** will need some 'continuous lighting'. This means studio lights that stay on all the time, as opposed to flash lighting used in still photography. You will need a minimum of two lights – and ideally three.

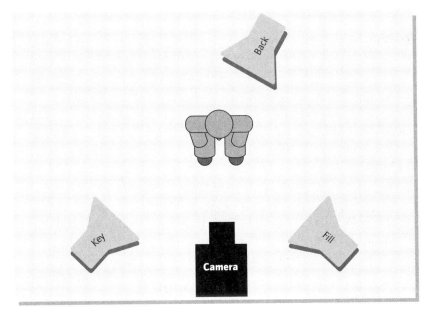

figure 8.2 Three-point lighting

For a professional studio look, use three-point lighting, arranged as shown in the diagram. Your main or 'key' light is the primary lighting source for your subject. The second light is to fill in the shadows, and should be used with a diffuser. The third light is above and slightly behind your subject's head, and separates him or her from the background with a halo of light. You will see this technique used on any TV show with talking-head punditry – look out for it.

Film a studio-based interview

A studio-based interview is the best way to have full control over the sound and lighting conditions, and create a professional-looking piece. Now, when I say 'studio', I don't mean you have to hire a TV studio. Any quiet room where you won't be disturbed will do – your office, a room you hire, even a location such as a trendy bar that you can hire out for a few hours. Your location should suit the tone of your video.

> 66 your location should suit the tone of your video 55

Lights Set up your three-point lighting as described above. If there are windows, keep the blinds or curtains open, unless bright sunlight is interfering with your shot. If there are lights in the room, switch them all on. Use all available light as well as your studio lighting.

Camera Use a tripod to steady your camera. Set the focus manually by zooming right in on your subject's nose, adjusting the focus until it's sharp, then zooming back out again. With all your lights on, set the 'white balance' by asking your subject to hold a piece of white paper in front of their face. Zoom in until this fills the screen. Set the white balance according to your camera's instructions, and zoom out again. This removes any 'colour cast' from artificial lighting, and ensures the colours in your finished video will be correct.

Action! If you are interviewing someone – such as a client, a colleague, or an expert in a particular field – you can either prime them with a few questions to respond to beforehand; or ask them questions from behind the camera (you asking the questions can be edited out later). Make sure you gather all the video material you will need to edit from later. Depending on how scripted the piece is, how fluent the speaker is, and how many takes you need, I would suggest you need up to half an hour of footage to create a 3–5 minute final piece.

The rule of thirds

Photographers often use the 'rule of thirds' to compose shots. This works well for filming interviews too. It just looks odd if the subject is in the middle of the screen. Instead, imagine the screen is divided into nine equally sized segments – three across and three down.

figure 8.3 The rule of thirds

Position your subject so that they're caught in the top-left or top-right crosshairs of these imaginary lines. Right between the eyes!

Styles can be:

▪ **A piece direct to camera** – the subject looks directly at the camera and says their piece. This isn't really an interview (though there might be someone prompting with questions from behind the camera), but it might be appropriate for filming a welcome message for your website.

▪ **Responses to an 'invisible director'** – the director or camera operator asks questions from behind and to one side of the camera. The subject looks at the director, NEVER at the camera. This creates a more professional image, and is the style you will see most commonly on documentaries and 'talking heads' shows.

▪ **An interview with a visible interviewer** – this is a more documentary style where the interviewer asks the subject questions on camera.

■ **A discussion** – where there are two or three subjects having a discussion about a set topic. It is best if this is unscripted, but essential that the participants are clear about the topics to be covered, and a 'pre-discussion' is useful before the camera rolls (though you may film this too as there could be usable footage). Subjects should generally not look at the camera, though sometimes treating the camera as an extra person in the conversation can work.

Using cutaways, noddies and B-roll

Where you have more than one person on camera, it is more interesting to show reaction shots and use close-ups of individuals speaking than a continuous mid-shot of everyone. Because of the small screen size most people will see the video on, close-up head shots will also be more visible than a group of people.

You can do this with a single camera by filming 'noddies' – reaction shots of the interviewer or other participants in a discussion nodding or listening intently to what others are saying. These can be filmed after the discussion. For close-ups of individual speakers, you will need to re-record parts of the discussion with different camera angles and zoom. This can feel unnatural for the speakers, especially if they are new to being filmed! But it comes out in the edit. Bear in mind at all times what you want the end result to look like, and that will guide you as to what footage you are going to need to get for the edit.

> **❝ bear in mind at all times what you want the end result to look like ❞**

The other reason for using noddies and other camera angles is that they can be used to cover up edits. You will probably want to use only parts of the footage you gather, and don't want the edits to jump and jar. Cut away to a reaction shot or close-up to cover up those jumps. This will work because you will be editing to the soundtrack – i.e. you will edit the complete final audio track first, and then add the correct pieces of film to it. The other way to cover edits is with 'B-roll'. This was traditionally additional footage shot by an extra, 'B' camera, such as establishing shots of the location of the shoot. You can film all of this with the same camera of course.

You might also use stock video footage where it seems appropriate to the topic being discussed and illustrates a point. For example, if the interviewee is talking about her cake decorating business, you could film separate footage later of her decorating cakes, or you might be able to use more generic stock footage of cakes being decorated. Does that sound a random, far-fetched example? There is plenty of affordable stock video footage on the Internet. I just did a search for cake decoration on www.istockphoto.com and found 68 video clips.

Edit and output your video

A full explanation of video editing goes beyond the scope of this book. The most important advice is that you should always use timeline-based video editing software. This means that you can add your soundtrack, music, video footage, images, titles, captions, effects and transitions to a single timeline and have a much greater degree of control. I recommend Final Cut Express for the Mac, and Adobe Premiere Elements for the PC. These cut-down versions of the software are much cheaper than the full versions and perfectly fine for your needs. You are not making a feature film, after all.

Create your soundtrack first. Most video editing software allows you to do this, though I prefer to edit it using Audacity first, as I would for audio podcasts. Once you're happy with your soundtrack, you can start adding your video to it, using noddies, cutaways and B-roll to cover the edits. You can also add images to your video, and should start and end with a 'slate' screen – a static image that might include a title, your company logo or a URL. The final screen should normally be your web address, since this will be the call to action – to visit your website.

66 once you're happy with your soundtrack, you can start adding your video 99

Once you've finished editing your video, you need to 'encode' it in a standard video format. You will find a number of preset options for this in your video editing software, which now often include presets optimised for YouTube, video podcasts, or web use.

Producing online video without a camera

Yes, you can still produce useful videos for your target audience without investing in any camera equipment at all – just some affordable software. If your business lends itself to online tutorials – i.e. showing people how to do things online – you can produce these using screen capture software such as Camtasia (www.techsmith.com/camtasia for PC or www.techsmith.com/camtasiamac for Mac). This can be useful for showing people how to use your online product. It's what I use to create the video tutorials for this book.

If your business doesn't sell online products that need explaining to clients, but you still have some knowledge to impart, you could do this by capturing PowerPoint slides and/or still images instead of websites, and add your own voiceover. If you do have a camera, you could even intersperse these with some pieces to camera. If you don't, you could use some stock video footage that illustrates your point. There is a wealth of cheap stock video clips at www.istockphoto.com.

Share your video

Just because YouTube is the biggest doesn't necessarily mean it is the right video-sharing site for your business. There are around 50 alternatives; plus you can also upload and share video on social networks such as Facebook and MySpace, and on sites that are usually thought of as photo-sharing sites such as Flickr. You can also upload video ads to your Google AdWords campaign.

Some of the main video-sharing sites are as follows.

Site	Description
YouTube (www.youtube.com)	This is still most likely to be your first port of call, since it is the most popular video-sharing site on the Internet, with over one billion views per day. You can upload videos of up to 10 minutes in length – but shorter is better.
Vimeo (www.vimeo.com)	Vimeo has over 2 million members, and prides itself on having the highest-quality video on the Internet. It is positioned more as a community of creative video producers, and does not allow you to upload commercials, infomercials, or demos that actively sell or promote a product or service – unless you work in a creative industry and want to use it to promote your work. That includes filmmakers, authors, musicians and actors.
Blip.tv (http://blip.tv)	Blip.tv has a different business model and a firm focus on content. It is worth a look if you want to make revenue from your video rather than simply use it as a promotional tool. Users create 'shows' which Blip.tv syndicate widely, including to YouTube, Vimeo and iTunes. Revenue is based on advertising and depends on audience size. It is split 50/50 between content creators and Blip.tv. As of August 2009 it claimed 48,000 'show creators', 2.4 million episodes and 22 million viewers.
12seconds.tv (http://12seconds.tv)	As the name suggests, this is for short, 12-second video clips and messages uploaded via web cam or mobile phone.
TwitVid (www.twitvid.com)	TwitVid is one of the video services aimed at Twitter users. Clips can be uploaded and automatically tweeted to your account. Videos can be favourited, commented on and embedded in the same way that YouTube videos can. Useful for ad hoc video uploads on the move.

As with any tool you use, it should be an appropriate channel for getting your message across, and where your content is likely to be found by your target audience.

Create a useful video resource for your audience without producing a single video

- Create a YouTube channel by going to www.youtube.com/create_account.

- Choose a username that matches your business, or has keywords related to your business.

- Be sure to include some details about your business, and your web address, in your profile (www.youtube.com/account#profile/about).

- Brand it to your business by editing the design and colour scheme of your channel at www.youtube.com/profile?edit=1. If you want to go a stage further, create a customised, branded background for your channel.

- Use the search box to find videos that you think will be of interest to your target market. These might be video tutorials, conference speeches, or information relevant to your industry. If you are a plumber, do a search for 'plumbing', and you'll be amazed at the range of videos on plumbing tips and repairs available!

- 'Favourite' a number of videos. Click on your some of your search results to play them, then select 'favorites' from the 'Save to' drop-down menu underneath the video. This will add it to your favourites list on your YouTube channel.

You now have a YouTube channel, some useful content to share with people, and a new way for people to find your business online. Ideally you will create and upload some of your own videos here, and then embed them back in your own website or blog. But meanwhile, you have a presence on YouTube.

Manage the workload

The work involved in creating online video is in producing it in the first place, rather than the maintenance. It may be something you do relatively infrequently compared with, say, blogging. But you should still check in to your YouTube channel periodically to favourite a few videos, and respond to friend requests and comments. Ways to maximise your effectiveness while minimising the work include:

- Whenever you film interviews, do several in one day if you can, so that you only have to set up and break down your equipment once. This is often the most time-consuming part, after editing.

■ Use a Twitter-based video-sharing service such as TwitVid for ad hoc videos on the move that can be linked automatically to your Twitter profile.

■ Sign up to YouTube email alerts so that you know whenever someone comments on your video without having to monitor the site.

■ Use the YouTube Autoshare feature (http://www.youtube.com/account#sharing/activity) to link your YouTube activities to your Twitter and/or Facebook accounts. These can include uploading, favouriting and commenting on videos.

■ Include your YouTube channel in the social media aggregator www.friendfeed.com, and then import this feed into Facebook using the FriendFeed app (http://apps.facebook.com/friendfeed), or into your blog or website using the widget supplied by FriendFeed.

■ Use a Facebook app such as YouTube Box (http://apps.facebook.com/videobox/) to include your YouTube videos on your Facebook page or profile.

Measure your results

There are plenty of basic statistics on video-sharing sites you can record, such as the number of views, ratings, and comments on your videos. But there are additional metrics and demographic data that you can access simply by clicking the down arrow next to the number of views. You can see these for any video, not just your own. The stats for the Blendtec iPad giveaway video are shown in Figure 8.4.

That will tell you something about who your videos are popular with and where. But you can go a stage further and measure who took action as a result of watching your video. By using a unique URL – a web address that is only ever mentioned on a specific video – you will be able to tell how many people have not only watched your video but also responded to your call to action. A unique URL can refer on to wherever you actually want the viewer to land – but you will be able to see from your web stats how many people took this journey.

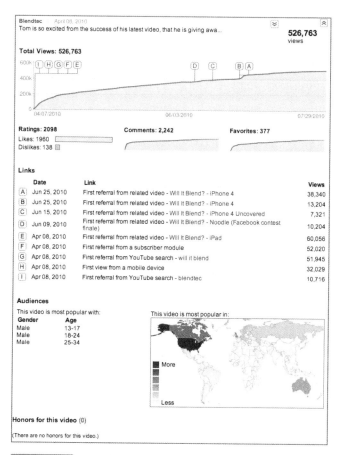

figure 8.4 YouTube metrics

You can use a unique URL in the description of your YouTube video – but it makes sense to also use it in the video itself, such as in a caption or on the end slate screen, so that it is visible when the video is embedded in another site.

You can do a similar thing with promotional codes that are used on a specific video. You will know how many people came to your site and bought something as a result of watching your video from the promo code used. This is useful if one of your goals for using video is to generate sales, since it is a direct measure of sales success.

If you don't want to use unique URLs or just want a more general idea of the effectiveness of your videos in driving traffic to your site, you can still discover a lot from your web analytics. Measure your traffic before and after you use video, and look at where the traffic is coming from.

If one of your goals is to reduce customer support queries, take a measure of the number of these before and after you use videos offering product demos or other customer support.

If your goal is raising brand awareness, you will need to use slightly more traditional means to discover your effectiveness, and conduct market research into your brand perception, including questions about where people first heard about you.

Take action

■ **Create** a YouTube Channel for your business at www.youtube.com/ create_account.

■ **Search** YouTube for videos in your business area.

■ **Favourite** some videos, and link these to Twitter/Facebook.

■ **Define** your business goals and choose a style of online video.

■ **Choose** your equipment.

■ **Film** an interview.

■ **Edit**, output and share your first video!

9

Show, don't tell
How to showcase your business on photo-sharing sites

Various sites allow you to upload and share your photos with others, either publicly or privately, including Flickr, Picasa, Photobucket, Snapfish and Blipfoto, plus services such as Twitpic and Tweetphoto that allow you to share images on Twitter. You can also share images on Facebook and MySpace. You may be familiar with some of these for sharing your personal or family photos. But they can also be used for business.

What is photo sharing?

Photo sharing is the uploading and sharing of your images on a third-party website. Most are free, at least to use a basic account with limited storage space. Most allow members to comment on each other's images, and members to 'tag' their images with keywords to aid searching. Images can often be rated and favourited, and members normally have a profile page with more information about them. This is usually the one place where you are allowed to mention your business, and link to it.

Why does photo sharing work for business?

❝ photo sharing works best if you have a visual element to your business ❞

Photo sharing works best if you have a visual element to your business that people are likely to search for on the photo-sharing sites they use. It is probably less useful for a service industry, such as accountancy. For example, if you run a hotel in a scenic part of the country, uploading local images will make you findable by people searching for that location. If you run a pet store, there are currently 12,460 Flickr groups dedicated to pets!

Like other forms of social media, photo sharing works best if you get involved in the community. Just as you can increase your visibility in the blogosphere by commenting on other people's posts, you will be more visible if you comment on other people's photos, add them to your 'favourites' and take part in discussions within groups. Every time you do this, your screen name will show. If that is your business name or web address, that is free advertising. Seek out images in your area of interest that get a lot of views to comment on. But don't do a hard sell – try to keep the conversation focused on the images.

---

photo sharing in action

Oxjam Music Festival (www.oxfam.org.uk/oxjam)

Oxjam is a music event organised in the UK each year by the charity Oxfam. Actually, it's really organised by hundreds of music lovers across the UK, who put together local music events throughout October, and donate the proceeds to Oxfam to help fight poverty. Active on Twitter, Facebook and MySpace (which has found its niche in music), Oxjam also has a Flickr group at www.flickr.com/groups/oxjam with over 2,300 photos taken by around 100 members across the UK.

Tagged with 'Oxjam' and uploaded to the group pool, they are a way of visually promoting the event. The group page includes a clear explanation of what Oxjam is, a call to action to 'get involved', and links not only to their website but also to their presence on other social sites. It helps promote their message, drive traffic to their website, engage supporters, and make an otherwise unmanageable amount of photography possible by crowdsourcing it as 'user-generated content'.

Get the idea: Encourage user-generated content (UGC) by setting up a Flickr group pool and encouraging people to post to it. This will engage your audience *and* cut down on your workload. You can then also pull these images back into your blog or website using a widget.

Together with uploading some great photos of your own, this social activity will lead people on to your profile page – which is the one place you really can sell yourself. Use this to write about your business and link to your website – but keep other commercial activity on Flickr to a minimum. Flickr's terms of service don't allow you to sell things directly, use it as a product catalogue, or include overtly sales-oriented messages or links in titles, tags, descriptions or comments. Using Flickr in this way could result in your account being deleted. More to the point, it's not a very smart way to use it. Better to think of Flickr – and other photo-sharing sites – as a community-building platform, a way to engage and involve your customers through sharing and commenting on photos.

Choosing a photo-sharing site

I tend to recommend Flickr, but other photo-sharing sites are available (see table overleaf). I am occasionally asked 'Which is better: Flickr or Twitpic?' The answer is 'It depends.' The services are so different, it depends what you want to do with your images.

You can, of course, also create albums and share photos on Facebook and MySpace. For example, my photographer, Krystyna Fitzgerald-Morris, uses MySpace to showcase her work and generate leads (www.myspace.com/krysbabooshkat).

Get up to speed with photo sharing

We will focus on Flickr for the rest of this chapter, since it offers the most potential for marketing your business with social media. The steps to follow are:

1 Sign up for an account with Flickr.
2 Upload some photos.
3 Use Flickr groups.
4 Link to your blog or website.

Sign up for an account with Flickr

Flickr is owned by Yahoo, and you will need a Yahoo login to get started – but this can be set up easily within minutes. It is free, or $24.95 (about £16) for a 'Pro' account with unlimited storage.

Think carefully about the username you choose. Do you want to use your personal name or business name? For a business account, unless your business is intimately tied to you as a person, I'd go for a business name.

Site	Users	Description	Business use
Flickr (www.flickr.com)	26m	In October 2009, Flickr claimed to host over four billion images. It also allows video sharing. Images can be organised into sets and collections, tagged with keywords, geotagged, and you can pull your latest images into your blog, website or Facebook page with widgets. Groups allow for postings from multiple users.	Although overt commercial use of Flickr is against their terms of service, you can still use it to engage your community online and lead them back to your website. Encourage user-generated content by setting up a Flickr group for people to submit images to – then pull them into your business website with a widget.
Picasa (http://picasa.google.com)	500K	Google's digital image sharing website. Includes image editing, geotagging, name tagging and face recognition software. Create slideshows, collages and 'web albums'.	Limited business use, except for photo storage and basic image editing.
Photobucket (http://photobucket.com)	50m	The only site that has free unlimited storage.	Limited business use, except for photo storage.
Snapfish (www.snapfish.com)	50m	Allows uploading and sharing of images, and ordering of prints and other items such as calendars, mugs and photobooks created from your images. This feature is now also possible via Flickr, which has a business partnership with Snapfish.	Less obvious business use – unless you use it to create photo-based merchandise!
Blipfoto (www.blipfoto.com)	unknown	A site that encourages you to keep a daily photo journal and upload a picture a day. Integrates with Twitter and Facebook.	Business use is prohibited – Blipfoto is for photography enthusiasts only. However, you can link to your own website from your profile. And if your business is photography, it's a good place to be. Stills (see Chapter 5) upload a daily image at www.blipfoto.com/stills, for example.
Twitpic (http://twitpic.com) Tweetphoto (http://tweetphoto.com)	unknown	Twitpic, Tweetphoto and similar services are for sharing pictures on Twitter – and can be a great way to enhance your use of Twitter, especially via a smartphone, which these automatically integrate with.	Add interest to your business Twitter account by tweeting images of what you're doing – especially if it is business related such as of your latest product, or your stand at a trade fair.

❝ you could even use your business web address as your screen name ❞

You can choose a different screen name to the one you use as for your username (which shows up in your Flickr URL), so you could even use your business web address as your screen name. That way, it will show up on every photo you upload.

Include some description of yourself and your business on your profile – and make sure you include a profile photo, or 'buddy icon' – it's a real turn-off on Flickr if you don't! This could be your company logo.

Upload some photos

Once you've joined, adding photos to Flickr is done through a simple upload system via the site. You can organise your images into themed 'sets', and your sets into themed 'collections' on your account. An alternative to setting up a dedicated business account is to use your personal account, and create a set, collection or group for your business images.

Upload good-quality images that are relevant to your business, such as:

- Photos of you or your staff in action – giving a seminar, arranging flowers, rewiring a house, catering events, selling sweets, making furniture – whatever it is that you do.

- Images of your products – although you should avoid using Flickr as a product catalogue, there's no reason not to include some quality photos of your cakes, wine, jewellery, etc. – and it is likely you will find Flickr groups relating to your specific product that you should also add these images to.

- Images of any events, workshops or seminars you run. For example, Chicago-based web design and development agency Headstand Media use Flickr to upload photos from their evening seminars at www.flickr.com/photos/headstandmedia.

Essential things to do when adding photos include:

- **Title it** – IMG0001254.jpg doesn't tell us anything. Give your image a descriptive title.

- **Tag it** – give your photo some descriptive tags, one of which should be your business name.

- **Describe it** – add as much description as you need to tell us what is going on, but avoid a sales pitch – focus on the photography, not the sale.

■ **Geotag it** – this is essential for any business where location is important, such as tourism, travel or real estate. But it is also useful for any business with a physical location. This is a subtle way to help people find you without being overtly promotional: upload some pictures of your restaurant, geotag them, and then people can click on the 'Map' link that appears next to your photo to find you! Be sure to include the name of the location in your tags too.

All these things will help your photos to be found in Flickr, and in search engines. In addition, decide on the level of visibility for your image, and how it can be used. You can set account defaults for these, but also amend them for any individual image any time.

■ **Public or private?** You can make photos visible to everyone, just to you, or just to friends and/or family. You choose who you add to your friends and/or family lists when you add people as contacts on Flickr. Generally, you want all your pictures to be publicly visible to everyone. But there might be occasions when you just want some visible only to you and/or colleagues. Or you might use the same account for personal as well as business photos, and just want the business ones to be public.

■ **Copyright or Creative Commons?** The default on Flickr is that you own the copyright to all your images, and '© All Rights Reserved' is displayed next to them. You can, however, change this, and opt for Creative Commons. This has emerged as an alternative to copyright, and means you can allow others to use your image so long as they use it in the way you want – such as for non-commercial use, unmodified, and with a credit. Newspapers and magazines do search Flickr for images – and using CC makes it more likely that yours will be used. Likewise, you can do a search for CC images, and use them on your own blog – so long as you credit the photographer and link back to the original image.

Batch process your uploads, or upload on the move

Use the Flickr 'Uploadr' – a small piece of software you can download and use to upload batches of images from your hard drive any time, without even being on the site (see http://www.flickr.com/tools). You can also batch-process adding titles, tags and descriptions, and automatically add your batch to an existing collection – or create a new one.

As with most social media tools, you can also use your mobile phone, and there is a Flickr iPhone app. Use this when you're out and about to capture relevant images and upload them on the move.

Use Flickr groups

Search for Flickr groups to join in your topic area. There are plenty of groups for anything you can imagine. Do you sell cakes? There are about 6,000 groups for that! If you are a local business, there is probably a group for your town or city too, which will help you reach a local audience.

❝ joining groups is the main way to raise awareness of your images ❞

Observe the group posting rules, which vary from group to group and are set by the group administrator. But then get uploading. Joining groups is the main way to raise awareness of your images. Be sure to take part in any forum discussions in your chosen groups, and comment on other members' photos – particularly those that get a lot of views.

The other option is to create your own group. You might create a group for your business that only you post to; or you could create an open group that others can post to. This is a more engaging way to build connections, and encourages user-generated content – and therefore cuts down on your workload. This approach would be suitable for any events or seminars that you organise. You can also include discussion forums in your group, an additional way of communicating with and engaging your members.

For example, Media140 organise conferences and events around the world on the future and impact of the 'real-time web', such as Twitter. As you would expect, there is plenty of tweeting at these events. But the collaborative media generation around these events also includes photos. A Flickr group at www.flickr.com/groups/media140 enables delegates to add their own photos. Including the tag 'media140' in their photos provides an additional way for people to find images of the events – even if they haven't been added to the group. The group page, like a Flickr profile page, allows for some promotional blurb about Media140 and a link to their website.

Link to your blog or website

Once you have a Flickr account, pull relevant images from your Flickr account or group into your website or blog using a widget. You can find a couple of these at www.widgetbox.com/widget/flickr-badge and www.widgetbox .com/widget/flickr-slideshow. There are also various WordPress plugins you can use on your blog, and Flickr apps you can use on your Facebook profile or page (see pages 76 and 147).

As well as adding some images and interest to your website, this gives people who are already on Flickr the opportunity to click through and add you as a contact, or see the rest of your images. It is another way to build a community around your business by going where your customers are.

You should link prominently from your website to your Flickr photostream whether or not you use a widget. This helps Google to follow the link from your website to your photos and index them too, thus increasing your search engine matches.

Measure your results

If you have a Flickr Pro account, you get access to loads of statistics on your account. Just go to 'Your Stats' under the 'You' menu to see a graph of views of your account over time and find out your most viewed photos.

You can also see where your traffic is coming from, such as from Google image search, in the Referrers list, and a handy breakdown of all your photos and videos on Flickr. You can even download all your stats as a text file.

Finally, if you want to measure click-throughs to your website as a result of your activity on Flickr, make your weblink from your profile page a unique URL that refers on to your site.

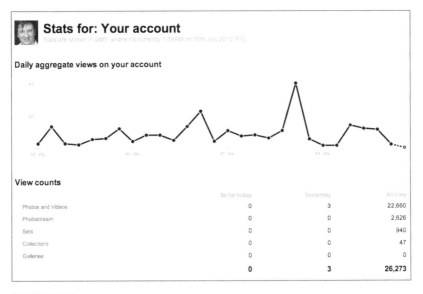

Take action

■ **Set up** an account at at www.flickr.com.

■ **Create** a profile, making sure you include a link to your website.

■ **Upload** some images.

■ **Join** groups relevant to your topic, add your images and join the discussions.

■ **Embed** your photos back on your blog or website with a widget.

part four

Get out there

Build a community

How to choose and use social networks

I f blogging has made everyone a publisher, social networking has made everyone a celebrity. Social networking sites have revolutionised the way we use the Web. On today's Internet, if you don't have what William Gibson calls a 'home-built media persona', you don't exist. And if your business doesn't have a presence on social networks, you're missing a massive opportunity to reach people where they are. Where once we emailed, now we network. And we spend a lot of our time doing it – one in every six minutes of online time is now spent on a social networking site.

❝ where once we emailed, now we network ❞

In this chapter, we shall look at the case for social networking, and some principles that apply whichever one you choose. The social networks that are likely to be of most benefit to your business are Facebook, LinkedIn and Twitter, and we shall look at these in more depth in the following chapters.

What is social networking?

Although there is a proliferation of social networking sites, most share some common features, including the ability to:

- Create a personal profile with some information about yourself, usually including a website and a profile image or 'avatar'.
- Update your 'status' – a short description of what you're doing.

■ Add friends to your list of contacts.

■ Set up a group, page or list of people for your area of interest.

■ Create and manage events.

■ Add and share photos and video.

■ Add extra functions through 'applications'.

■ Promote your product or service with advertising.

Many social networks can also be used as 'aggregators' – they can be linked together, so status updates from other networks, plus your blog posts and other content items can appear in the same place. This can save you a lot of maintenance time, since what you do on one site can show up on several others automatically.

Why social networking works for business

Social networking works for business because you can build connections, build a list, build word of mouth, and build trust. All are key to your online marketing success, and nothing beats social networks for making it happen.

Build connections Do you go to real-life business networking events, armed with a fistful of business cards? Do you have lots of enthusiastic conversations with people who you never hear from again? Or do you come away with solid business leads for new prospects and suppliers? Either way, this process is compressed and multiplied online.

Like real-life networking, you can meet people and start conversations. You can provide helpful advice, and ask for it. Unlike real-life networking, you don't have to do this one-to-one, but one-to-many. Very many. You can reach more people, all over the world, 24 hours a day, articulate your offering to them and collect their contact details without ever leaving your office. You can also become well known in your niche community, and the obvious 'go to' person on your area of expertise for the people you want to reach.

Build a list Your networks act as opted-in mailing lists you can use to reach highly targeted people who are likely to be interested in your product or service. They've sought you out and chosen to be on your list, after all.

Build word of mouth Having your product or service recommended to your potential customers by people they trust is called 'word of mouth' marketing – and is the Holy Grail of marketing. It becomes much easier to achieve this with the power of social networking. If you create content worth passing on, your fans will help market your business for

❝ word of mouth is the Holy Grail of marketing ❞

you. For example, if someone becomes a fan of your Facebook page, that will show up on their profile page, and in the news feeds of their friends – some of whom may click on the link and become a fan too.

Likewise, if your video is compelling enough for someone to share on their profile page, or your blog post interesting enough for someone to link to or retweet on Twitter, that too becomes more visible and helps spread the word. In this way, media, marketing and people all get mixed up together.

Build trust As well as getting your message passed on to new people by people they trust – something that applies to all forms of social media – social networks help build trust in you too. People like to do business with people they know; and mediating yourself via a social network is a great way for people to get to know you. You don't have to fill your MySpace page or Facebook profile with lots of business information – though a clear link to your business website is a must. Just be yourself, and include information about your business where appropriate. Don't use it as a sales channel only, though. People like to see a well-rounded, authentic individual with diverse interests – not a faceless corporate clone.

---

social networking in action

Ivy Ellen Wedding Stationery (www.ivyellen.co.uk)

Jeremy Corner set up Ivy Ellen in October 2009, a Brighton-based wedding stationery business, and quickly grew the brand using social networking. Using a range of social networks, particularly Facebook, Twitter and LinkedIn, they have built up a wealth of useful leads, contacts – and business.

Each network is used differently: LinkedIn for professional contact with wedding suppliers such as venues, photographers, dressmakers and wedding planners; Facebook for more customer-focused special offers, wedding freebies and funny wedding stuff; and Twitter for more frequent updates – fun, friendly wedding tips, facts and news. Twitter is their most successful social media tool at present for driving traffic and growing brand awareness.

They have also experimented with Facebook Social Ads, Google AdWords, bridal shows and wedding magazine PR, and track everything using special offer codes and even different 0845 numbers that tell them which calls come from which campaigns. Google Analytics help measure which social networks work best for them.

Their use of social networking has led to several blogs and articles being written about them; sales leads, brand champions referring them to others, building incoming weblinks, industry knowledge, sales orders and substantial brand awareness in a short space of time. In the six months following launch, the company was growing at 140 per cent per month.

Their key to success is being organised about it, and setting aside time for marketing. Jeremy says: 'You should focus on spending at least a third of your time marketing – more for a new business in my view'. They use a number of third-party tools to help manage the time spent on Twitter, including filtering and scheduling tweets with Hootsuite (http://hootsuite.com). 'I believe the future of search will be social', he continues, 'so I consider it time well spent, and I value my time highly as I only work three days per week and run three separate businesses. I would not be growing the Ivy Ellen brand as fast without these tools.'

Jeremy advises business owners to think of social networking as their ultimate online referral system: 'If you are consumer facing, social media is a must-have in your toolbox. Just as you should think about what value your business offers your customers, think about what value you can offer your followers. Be helpful, be funny or be informative. Most people will enjoy following and interacting with you if you do these things.'

Get the idea: Use several social networks, but use each in a way appropriate to the platform and its audience. Set aside time for social networking, and use tools such as http://hootsuite.com and www.tweetdeck.com to help manage it. Focus on the value you can offer, and your follower numbers will increase.

Top 12 social networking sites

The top 12 social networks, in order of size are as follows. Some may surprise you, some may be new to you – and not all will be suitable for your business:

Social network	Users	Description	Business use
Facebook (www.facebook.com) See Chapter 11.	500m	The largest and most geographically spread general social network. Find the latest statistics at http://www.facebook.com/press/info.php?statistics.	Great for creating opted-in mailing lists using pages and groups, finding your niche community of interest, engaging them with content and drawing them on to your website.
QZone (http://qzone.qq.com)	200m	Second largest by number of users, but restricted to mainland China.	Useful if you do business in China.
Habbo (www.habbo.com)	162m	A general social networking site for teenagers. Formerly Habbo Hotel.	Worth a look if your business is aimed at teenagers, but not really a business-oriented network.
MySpace (www.myspace.com)	130m	MySpace tends to have a slightly younger demographic, and has found its niche in the promotion of music and other creative work.	Use MySpace if you are a creative professional, such as a musician, artist, filmmaker or photographer.
Windows Live Spaces (http://home.spaces.live.com)	120m	Microsoft's blogging and social networking platform. Formerly MSN Spaces.	More suited to personal blogging.
Orkut (www.orkut.com)	100m	Owned by Google, and popular in India and Brazil.	Worth considering if you are based in, do business in or target these specific geographic markets.
Friendster (www.friendster.com)	90m	Popular in Southeast Asia, but not as popular as it once was in the West.	

▶

Social network	Users	Description	Business use
Hi5 (http://hi5.com)	80m	Created and headquartered in the USA, but more popular in other countries, especially Latin America.	
Vkontakte (http://vk.com/index.php)	75m	The largest website in the Russian-speaking world, and the most popular social network in Russia, Ukraine, Belarus and Kazakhstan. Has a very similar interface to Facebook, and is often considered a clone of the site.	
Twitter (http://twitter.com) See Chapter 13.	75m	I consider Twitter more of a social network than a 'microblogging' site, since people use it in a more social way these days.	Great for building up an opted-in list of 'followers', and engaging your community with a useful news feed in your area of expertise. Also useful for quick updates, latest news and time-limited discount codes. Business and personal accounts both welcome.
Tagged (www.tagged.com)	70m	California-based social network initially aimed at teens, but with a more adult demographic now.	A general social network, but not really a business-oriented network. A fraction of the size and less well-known than Facebook.
LinkedIn (www.linkedin.com) See Chapter 12.	70m	A business-oriented social network – a combination of an online CV/résumé and business contact list. Since 2009 has included additional functions such as groups, events and integration with Twitter.	An essential business tool. More useful for developing professional contacts, or for lead generation for B2B businesses. Less useful for consumer-facing businesses. Can also be a great way of promoting your business blog by pulling it into the news section of your LinkedIn group.

Which social network?

There are lots of social networking sites out there. Which do you choose? Do you just sign up to as many as possible and hope for the best? Do you pick the largest?

One factor is geography. It partly depends on where in the world you are. In the UK and the USA, Facebook dominates. In India and Brazil, Orkut is popular. Friendster used to be popular in the West, but is now most used in Southeast Asia. Hi5 is popular in places as diverse as Portugal, Thailand and Central Africa – but not in the USA.

The real deciding factor is to go where your market is, as with any social media tool. But a good guiding principle is to focus on the largest networks worldwide, those that are best suited to promoting your business, and choose one as your main network.

- Unless it is not widely used in your geographic region, make **Facebook** your main social network. Otherwise, establish a presence on the largest social network in the region(s) in which you do business.
- If you work in the creative industries – such as music or film – set up a profile on **MySpace**, which has found its niche in this area.
- If you want to target a younger demographic, **Habbo** is specifically for teens.
- Put your CV/résumé on **LinkedIn** – whether or not you use it for networking. It's a way to create an online résumé that you can link to from your website.
- Use **LinkedIn** more actively if you are a business-to-business (B2B) company.

You can set a profile on all of them of course, even if it is just a 'holding' page that directs people to your main social networking profile. But choose one as your main network, and set up a personal profile rather than a corporate-sounding brochure. We want personal information about you and your interests.

Do I need a personal profile?

What if you're just not comfortable with opening your personal diary to the world? Can't you just have, say, a Facebook page or group without creating a personal profile first?

Don't underestimate the power of personality and your personal brand. Your profile should be more than a sanitised corporate version of yourself. Human beings are more trusted than faceless businesses. The old distinctions of 'work life' and 'personal life' are breaking down. Work–life balance is giving way to work–life integration, where you're allowed to be a human being without upsetting business contacts. That doesn't mean you can be rude about your employer or your clients online! I have met people who think that's what authenticity means. It isn't.

> **your profile should be more than a sanitised corporate version of yourself**

If you or your employer is uncomfortable with your use of social networking profiles, remember that there are usually privacy settings that can be applied to specific groups of your friends. The other thing you may consider is setting up a separate 'work' profile specifically for the purpose of creating pages and groups that are used as your main social networking presence. You do, after all, need a profile on Facebook before you can create pages or groups. Do this with caution, though. If there are multiple versions of you on the same site, how will people know which one to connect to? Some people use a very basic profile for work, using their first name and company name: e.g. if you work for ABC Widgets, your profile name could be 'Jon ABC' or 'Jon ABC Widgets', and use your logo as your profile picture. It is important that it is clear that there is a real person behind the profile. This is not just to build trust, but because it is the way Facebook in particular should be used. Profiles are for people – not businesses or products.

LinkedIn is all about personal profiles, since the core of the site is your curriculum vitae (CV) or résumé online. On Twitter, both business and personal accounts are common. It can be helpful to have both. By all means use an account branded to your business, but consider also a personal Twitter account, and mention this in the biography section of your business account.

If you use several networks, be aware that your audience may be a little different on each, and provide appropriate content and information that they're likely to be interested in. In the next three chapters, we will look in more detail at Facebook (Chapter 11), LinkedIn (Chapter 12) and Twitter (Chapter 13).

Take action

▮ **Register** for accounts with **Facebook, LinkedIn** and **Twitter.**

▮ **Choose** your main social network(s). Which are the best fit with your business?

▮ **Consider** setting up a profile on other, 'secondary' networks.

Find fans on Facebook

How to harness the world's largest network

At the Toronto International Film Festival in 2009, George Clooney declared he would 'rather have a prostate exam on live television by a guy with very cold hands than have a Facebook Page'. Whether you would rather be poked by a medical doctor on television or by a friend on Facebook, there's no denying the reach of the world's largest social network. At the time of writing, Facebook has over 500 million active users, of whom half log on in any given day. You can see the latest statistics for yourself at www.facebook.com/press/info .php?statistics. But it is not size alone that makes Facebook a good place to do business: its functions and features lend themselves to finding your community of interest, and promoting your goods or services to them.

What is Facebook?

Facebook originally started as a college network in the USA. You had to have an American university email address to join. Since opening its doors to everyone in 2006, the demographic has rapidly aged and, in common with many social networks, the fastest-growing age group is people over the age of 35. Don't dismiss it as being for kids. Facebook has become one of the most widely used online marketing tools for business.

Why Facebook works for business

Alongside the usual personal profiles you would expect, Facebook offers a wide variety of tools such as pages, groups, events, applications and ads. Because it has such a large user base, you will almost certainly find a community of interest on Facebook, however niche your area. You can reach very specific, targeted users for little cost with 'social ads'. But the best thing is it's completely free to create a page or

❝ your customers are on Facebook – so you need to be ❞

group specifically for your business or product, and your target market will find it. A Facebook page is the single most important thing you can do on Facebook – and one of the easiest. There are more than 160 million pages, groups and events on Facebook, and the average user is connected to 60 of them. Your customers are on Facebook – so you need to be.

Facebook in action

Snapdragon (www.snapdragongarden.co.uk)

Jane Lindsey runs a small craft business in Scotland. She creates embroidered textiles, such as button badges and notebooks, and also prints them as greetings cards. She has moved from retail only, via her website and local fairs, to wholesale, and now stocks over 270 shops. Facebook has been key to her success. Jane says: 'For a small business without a marketing budget, Facebook allows me to connect with a large number of people for free.'

Snapdragon began as a very local business: 'I knew the vast majority of my customers personally', says Jane. 'It was more like a farm-gate type of business. When the business grew I wanted to keep that local element, to have customers feel that they knew me. I also wanted to get the story of the business out – that we make everything individually and there are no computerised sewing machines. Facebook allows me to do that – to post about the extended life of the business, be that the wildlife that surrounds us, new designs, or a great new stockist.'

Jane uses Facebook to publicise events that are going on at galleries that stock her work, and to have a meaningful dialogue with customers – both retail and wholesale. Over the past year 30 per cent of new business has come from either Facebook or Twitter. Jane says: 'One challenge in selling wholesale without using an agent is reminding shops to re-order. Facebook allows me to do that in a non-spammy way to the shops that follow me. In return the shops get to know about new products coming up.'

figure 11.1 Snapdragon profile page on Facebook

Get the idea: Use Facebook to tell your story and create a personal connection with people – not just with customers, but with wholesalers and suppliers too. Promote events, and use plenty of photos of your products. As Jane says: 'Don't try to sell, try to connect.'

Get up to speed with Facebook

In this section, we will look at the steps you need to take to get up to speed with Facebook.

1 Create your profile.
2 Create a page or group to build a community around your business.
3 Create an event to promote your business.
4 Set up a social ad to target your niche.

Optionally, you might also want to sell products using Facebook Marketplace (http://apps.facebook.com/marketplace).

Create your profile

If you are not yet on Facebook, the first step is to create a profile. That's the easy part: just sign up for an account and enter some information about yourself. You may not use your own personal profile to promote your business, unless you are the brand or very tied to the business, such as a consultant or musician; but you will need to have one in order to create groups, pages or events. Events can also be created by pages and groups.

1   If you don't have a personal profile, go to www.facebook.com and create one now.

2   Enter as much or as little personal information as you want in the fields provided on the Info tab, but you should always include your business website in the weblinks field. You can include multiple web addresses if you want – though too many may confuse people.

3   Be sure to add a profile picture so people know it's you.

4   The most important place to enter some information about yourself is in the small box beneath your profile image. This is likely to be the first thing that people read. You can enter 250 characters here, and it should be your 'elevator pitch' – a short, succinct articulation of what you do and the benefit you offer. Think of it as the online equivalent of introducing yourself to someone at a real-life business networking event as you hand them your business card. There is an 'Information' box beneath this. Click on the pencil icon (top-right) to edit which of the information from your Info tab appears here. At a minimum you should include your web address, so that anyone intrigued enough by your elevator pitch can click straight through to your business website. If you don't yet have a website or blog, you can enter the web address for another social network that you're on, or for your Twitter page.

5   Spend a bit of time getting your profile right before you start adding friends, but don't spend too much time on this beyond the basics – we will quickly be moving on to pages, groups and events.

6   Do a search for your topic area, and join a few groups and become a fan of (or 'Like') a few pages. This will help familiarise yourself with the possibilities, and give you some places where you can post messages and make more connections (though don't just spam groups with your marketing message!)

You can make your profile as visible or invisible as you like to whoever you choose using the privacy settings. If you are using your personal profile to develop new contacts and get business, you will probably want most people to be able to see it. But even if you choose a high level of privacy, you can still connect with as many people as you want on Facebook via a more public page.

Create a page or group

Groups and pages offer you a way of creating a fully opted-in mailing list: your members and fans have sought you out and chosen to join your group or become a fan of your page, making this the ultimate in permission-based marketing. You can have as many members or fans as you like, where profiles are limited to 5,000 friends. And, like profiles, pages and groups allow status updates, which show up in the news feeds of your fans or members. There are also differences between them, which are worth considering when planning your strategy.

Page or group?

Feature	Page	Group
Membership	Fans	Members
Functionality	Pages allow you to add many of the same applications that you can add to your profile, making pages the more powerful option to use in most cases.	Groups come with a basic set of functions, including photos, videos, events and discussions.
Discussion	Pages work best for promoting businesses or products in a more 'broadcast' way.	Groups are more useful for encouraging discussion between members.
Status updates	Appear as your page's logo and name, so is a little more anonymous, and can be updated by multiple people without causing confusion.	Appear written by you personally, with your profile page avatar and name.
Messaging	With pages, you can 'send an update to fans'. You can be more targeted, and just send an update to fans in a particular country, region or city, within a specific age range, or to just men or women. Unlike social ads – which allow even more specific targeting – this is free. However, this is a less visible method for reaching people, since these updates do not show up in the message inbox of your fans, but on their updates page, which is an extra click away.	Groups offer more powerful messaging, since you have an option to 'message all members' – effectively a mass mailing of a Facebook message to all the members of your group. These messages show up in their Facebook message inbox.
Measurement	One of the major advantages of pages over groups is the level of information and analytics about your fans that you have access to. We will look more at that in the 'Measure your results' section.	Limited to simple number of members.

Whether you choose a page or a group to promote your business – or both – be careful about your choice of name. In most cases this is likely to be your business name. But you could also go for a topic-based name. Either way, it helps to consider the name of your group or page as carefully as you would a domain name, since people will search for you by keywords on Facebook.

Create a group

1 Go to http://www.facebook.com/groups/create.php.

2 Enter a name and description for your group, and choose the most appropriate category from the drop-down menu. All these things will help people find your group, so think carefully about your group name and, where possible, include the search terms you expect people to use.

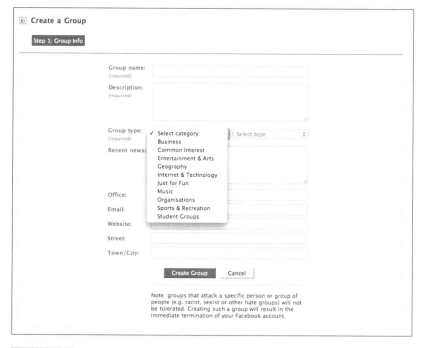

figure 11.2 Create a Facebook group

3 Include the other details requested, especially **website**, and click **Create Group**.

4 Continue customising your group as you wish.

Create a page

1 Go to http://www.facebook.com/pages/create.php, or scroll to the bottom of any Facebook page and click the 'Create a Page for My Business' link.

2 Choose whichever radio button applies to you: 'Local business', 'Brand, product or organization' or 'Artist, band or public figure'. There are additional subcategories to choose from in a drop-down menu that will appear.

3 Give your page a name, click the 'Create official Page' button, and continue customising.

4 Unlike groups, you can install most of the same applications (apps) that you have on your personal profile. We will look at these next.

figure 11.3 Create a Facebook page

Choose and install apps

1 Go to your Facebook Page, and click the **Edit Page** link underneath your logo/image.

From this administrative page, you can adjust your settings, create events, manage and install apps. You can also see your statistics by clicking on **Pages** at the top of the page and then **View Insights** for the page you're interested in.

2 Scroll to the bottom of the page to find the **More applications** box. Click on **Browse more** to search for applications.

3 The apps search function is not great – though you will often find more of the right sort of apps if you search under **Business** rather than **All Applications.**

Apps to consider

Name	URL	Description
Facebook Notes	http://www.facebook.com/notes.php	Pulls in blog/other RSS feed. One of the most useful ways you can enhance your page and keep the content fresh is by pulling in your blog. The standard Facebook Notes app is one of the best ways of doing this – just edit the settings in the admin interface you reach via your **Edit Page** link.
Blog RSS Feed	http://apps.facebook.com/blogrssreader/	
Social RSS	http://apps.facebook.com/social-rss/tabsettings.php	
My del.icio.us	http://apps.facebook.com/mydelicious	Displays your latest Delicious bookmarks (see Chapter 15).
My Flickr	http://apps.facebook.com/myflickr	Displays a selection of photos from your Flickr account. Specify which photos display by nominating a photoset, tags, most recent or most interesting.
YouTube Box	http://apps.facebook.com/videobox	Display your YouTube videos on your page.
Poll	http://apps.facebook.com/opinionpolls	Create a poll on your site – useful for product development.
Reviews	http://www.facebook.com/apps/application.php?id=6261817190	Allow your customers to review your products or services.
Twitter	http://apps.facebook.com/twitter	Turn your tweets into your Facebook status. Can be used on your personal profile or page, but not on both.
Selective Tweet Status	http://apps.facebook.com/selectivetwitter	Particularly useful for controlling which tweets go to your page or profile: only those tweets containing #fb will be pushed through to Facebook. It can also be used with multiple pages and Twitter accounts.
Facebook Page to Twitter	www.facebook.com/twitter	Cross-promote by pushing your Facebook page status update of up to 420 characters out to Twitter as a 120 character tweet plus bit.ly link back to your page.

quick win

Create your own Facebook application

The more adventurous way to benefit from Facebook applications is to create your own. You will need some programming skills, or to hire a developer, to create a bespoke application with lots of functionality that people can add to their own profiles. However, there is a simpler way to do it yourself.

There are several applications on Facebook that enables you to create a box on your profile or page that contains whatever HTML you want. These applications include:

▪ **My HTML.**

▪ **HTML Profile Box**. This can only be used on your profile.

▪ **Static FBML** (http://www.facebook.com/apps/application. php?id=4949752878). FBML stands for 'Facebook Markup Language' – but normal HTML works just fine to. This can be used on pages, and is my favourite because you can add as many boxes as you want to your page using this one application. You can also create a bespoke tab on your page.

If you, or someone you know, knows some basic HTML, that's great. But the main thing I would suggest using your own customised HTML box for an email newsletter sign-up form – and you can do that without any coding knowledge. If you set up your email marketing in Chapter 5, you should have a piece of code supplied by your email newsletter service provider. Simply paste the code into one of the Facebook HTML apps. If you don't yet have your email marketing set up, but have a blog, you could include links to subscribe to your blog by RSS or email instead.

The other app to consider is Application Builder (http://apps.facebook.com/ applicationbuilder). This allows you to create one of 13 different types of app, such as gifts, quizzes, polls and a fan page application that can be used to promote your page.

Five ways to win with Facebook pages

1 **Claim your username**. Once you have 25 fans, you claim your own 'vanity URL' instead of meaningless numbers. The Facebook page for this book is www.facebook.com/getuptospeed, for example. Claim yours at www.facebook.com/username.

2 **Import your blog**. The Notes app is the easiest way to do this, and keeps your page fresh.

3 **Integrate with Twitter.** You can import your Twitter status to your Facebook page status selectively using the Selective Tweet Status app. You can also *export* your page status to Twitter using the Facebook Page to Twitter app at www.facebook.com/twitter.

4 **Create a landing tab.** Use the Static FBML app to create a bespoke tab for your page. Then edit your wall settings on your 'edit page' screen to select the tab you want non-fans to land on. By doing this you can decide what people see before they become a fan, and tempt them in with compelling content.

5 **Promote your page.** Now that you've created a page let people know about it: blog about it, tweet about it and include it in your email signature. A great way to encourage people to 'like' your page direct from your blog or website is with a 'Like' button. Find this, and other 'social plugins' at http:// developers. facebook. com/plugins.

Create an event

Events are useful for product launches, conferences, seminars, etc., especially when you have many potential attendees as fans of your page or members of your group.

Events can be created by:

1 Individuals/profiles – http://www.facebook.com/events/create.php.

2 Groups – click on the **Create group event** link below your logo/ image.

3 Pages – click on the **Edit Page** link underneath your logo/image, then on the **Edit** link underneath **Events**.

Use social ads

'Social Ads' are what Facebook calls those ads you see on the right-hand side of your screen. I have my doubts about how effective they are, compared with engaging people with valuable content on your Facebook Page (have you clicked on one of those ads lately?) – and they cost money. However, social ads are worth considering for a short period when you first launch something – whether it's your website, your Facebook Page or a new product or service – to help raise awareness within your target audience.

> ❝ social ads are worth considering for a short period when you first launch something ❞

They are also worth considering because they are highly targeted – not only by demographics such as gender, location and age, but by the keywords and job titles people include in their profiles. You can reach a small number of highly targeted individuals for very little cost.

You have the option of choosing pay per click, or pay per view. Because click-through rates on Facebook are so low, you should always choose pay per click. Like other PPC services, such as Google AdWords, you can set a budget limit, and spend as much or as little as you choose.

The other reason to look at social ads – even if you have no intention of ever advertising on Facebook – is to research the size of your potential market on Facebook. If you go through the ad set-up screens but without actually completing your ad, you can still do the demographic and keyword targeting to find out how many people you *could* reach with an ad. As you narrow your keyword-based search criteria, Facebook will give you a number – the number of people at whom the ad would be targeted. This will provide you with some useful market intelligence about the people you are trying to reach. It is especially useful if you are a local business and may even help you decide if Facebook is a good place for you to do business.

Find out more at www.facebook.com/advertising.

Manage the workload

You can cut down on time maintaining groups and pages – especially if you have several – by setting up multiple administrators to look after them. These might be colleagues or employees, or a task outsourced to a virtual assistant. See Chapter 16 for more on hiring virtual assistants.

But the real trick to managing your Facebook workload is to *aggregate*. Social networking really starts to get interesting once you use Facebook as an aggregator for your social media presence elsewhere. Do this by installing some of the apps on your page that pull in your blog, videos, Flickr photos, Delicious links and so on.

You can go a stage further by signing up to another social network called FriendFeed (www.friendfeed.com). Don't worry – this isn't going to be yet another network that you have to maintain – you're just going to tell it the other social sites you have a presence on, and let it do the rest.

Although you can use FriendFeed to post status updates, send direct messages, create lists of friends and join groups, the most effective way to use it is simply as a social media aggregator: a place to create single timeline made up of all your feeds from various social sites.

With FriendFeed you can list around 60 different web services that you're on, including blogs and RSS feeds, social bookmarking sites, photo-sharing sites, status updates from Facebook and Twitter, video-sharing sites such as YouTube and many others. This is a way of really cutting down the maintenance workload. Whenever you add photos to Flickr, favourite a video on YouTube, update your blog, update your Twitter status and so on, it all appears in a real-time aggregated timeline on FriendFeed. And the best thing is that no one actually has to go to your FriendFeed page to see this. By installing the FriendFeed application on Facebook, all your updates from FriendFeed (and therefore your entire social media presence), will appear in your Facebook timeline. If you wish, you can also create a widget to put on your blog, or link FriendFeed to Twitter. FriendFeed offers a range of advanced Twitter settings that enable you to post everything to Twitter or just those specific services you choose. You can also choose to make the links click through to the original source instead of FriendFeed.

❝ this is a way of really cutting down the maintenance workload ❞

You probably won't want to rely exclusively on FriendFeed to aggregate your social media within Facebook, particularly if you have a blog or podcast that you want to make more prominent on your profile or page. You could include your FriendFeed feed on a discrete tab within your page, and rely on the range of Facebook applications that will pull in your most important media, such as your blog, on to your wall.

Measure your results

This is really where Facebook pages come into their own. You have free access to a vast amount of data and metrics about your fans. This can be useful for market research, developing new products or services, or just gaining a better understanding of who your customers are.

Simply go to www.facebook.com/pages/manage and click **View Insights** next to the page that you want to see the data for.

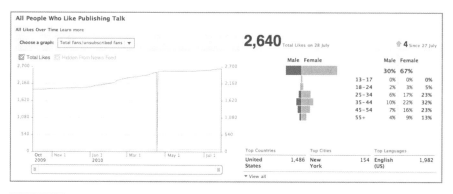

figure 11.5 Facebook insights

You can also go directly to www.facebook.com/insights to view data for all your pages. Data available include:

■ Demographic breakdown by age and gender.

■ Fourteen different graphs over time, including total fans, new fans, top.countries, interactions and mentions.

■ Breakdown of fans by geographic location – both by country and city. This is useful if, say, you're considering a local marketing campaign in cities where you're popular, or simply to target your social ads better.

■ Most popular languages used by fans. This might be useful for deciding whether you should make parts of your website available in other languages.

With groups, you have little more than the number of members to go on.

For social ads, you get the sort of statistics you would expect: impressions, click-through rates, traffic and costs. You should record these for each campaign you run, to get an idea of which are the most effective.

Take action

- **Sign** up for an account at www.facebook.com.

- **Set up** a personal profile.

- **Create** a page or group for your business.

- **Promote** your page.

- **Install** applications and consider creating your own app.

- **Aggregate** your other social media.

12

Create credibility on LinkedIn

How to take your business networking online

L inkedIn is more of a professional than a social network – which makes it ideal for business. It has an older demographic than many of the generic social networks, with an average age of 41. At the end of 2009, it had over 75 million users. Where Facebook users have friends and Twitter users have followers, LinkedIn users have contacts. Use it to develop business contacts, or to develop sales leads if you sell to other businesses.

What is LinkedIn?

LinkedIn has been around since 2003, and was initially little more than a place to keep an online version of your CV or résumé and make business connections – a bit like handing out business cards in cyberspace. It has since evolved into a more social tool, with integration with Twitter updates, applications that enable you to increase functionality such as pulling in a blog, and the ability to create events and groups. Many of the core functions you would expect in a generic social network like Facebook, but tailored for business. It's worth a look even if you just set up a profile then ignore it, since it's another place for people to find you. But you may be surprised by its marketing potential, particularly for business-to-business (B2B) marketing.

Why LinkedIn works for business

LinkedIn works for business in several ways.

> 66 LinkedIn is like a big business networking party where everyone is handing out business cards 99

Building business connections Whether it's getting back in touch with old colleagues or meeting new contacts, LinkedIn is like a big business networking party where everyone is handing out business cards, and saying 'You must meet my colleague X' or 'I'm looking for a graphic designer, can you recommend someone?' Use it to tell people what you do, but also for introductions and recruitment.

Unlike Twitter or Facebook, you can only send contact requests invitations to people you know, have some business connection with, whose email address you know, or who you have been introduced to via a mutual contact.

LinkedIn shows you your number of contacts – but, unlike Facebook, also calculates a number of potential contacts in your wider network of friends of friends. This is very powerful, as it is a database of professionals who are likely to be within your broad areas of interest, who you are not directly connected to, but to whom you could get an introduction via people you do know. This is like real-life business networking, except that you can see which people your business contacts know in front of you on your screen, and decide who you think might be useful for you to know, without any conversation taking place over cocktails and canapés (OK, that might be a downside!).

Positioning yourself as an expert One of the things people do on LinkedIn is ask questions of their extended business community. If you have an area of expertise you can share, you can use it to position yourself as an expert.

Promoting your business Like Facebook, you can join groups in your area of interest, and post relevant messages to them. You can also create adverts, though I find this less effective – and far more expensive. You can create groups to engage your community of interest and build up a following. Although you should avoid anything too spammy, marketing messages are much less frowned upon on LinkedIn. It's a business network – promoting your business on it is fine. Just keep it relevant to the people you're talking to.

Bear in mind at all times that your audience on LinkedIn may be subtly different from your audience on Facebook or Twitter. With all social networks, keep your status updates and postings relevant to your community of interest and the network you're communicating on.

LinkedIn in action

Linda Ruck Communications (LRC) (www.lindaruck.com)

If you're a self-employed business consultant, LinkedIn can be great not only for building contacts but also for winning contracts. Linda Ruck runs her own public relations and event management consultancy in Singapore, Linda Ruck Communications (LRC). LinkedIn has helped make her a global player. Writing on the LinkedIn blog[5], she says: 'Being a small business owner carving out a niche against the big players is very challenging. As with any small business you need to develop viable strategies, seek out opportunities and be creative on how to promote your business, all with a limited budget!'

For people working business-to-business, LinkedIn is an obvious route to market. Linda's profile has generated leads and clients from the USA, UK, Australia and throughout Asia from companies, including big multinationals, seeking an expert to run events, media and PR in Singapore and the region.

Linda's first success though LinkedIn was when she was hired by a multinational company based in Boston which required a PR consultant in Singapore to support their Asian expansion plans. The company searched LinkedIn to find a PR company in Singapore who had expertise dealing with US-based companies. She has since worked with the same company every time they have a project in the region. Many of her clients found her this way, simply by searching the site or through 'introductions', which is a feature that enables you to ask your contacts for an introduction to one of their contacts.

But Linda also participates in discussions in relevant LinkedIn Groups. This, together with LinkedIn Answers, is an excellent way to promote your expertise in a niche field, and increase your visibility on the network. Linda says: 'Groups is a great platform to engage in discussions and connect with like-minded professionals to learn and share, whether it's for business or personal interest. And, most importantly, helps establish my thought leadership in a space I've carved out for myself as a small business owner.'

---

5 http://blog.linkedin.com/2009/07/14/linda-ruck-helping-entrepreneurs-and-smb-owners-win-global-clients

> **Get the idea**: Because LinkedIn is a network built on business contacts and referrals, it works well for consultants, freelancers and independent professionals. Participate actively in LinkedIn Groups and Answers to build a reputation as an expert in your field. Solicit recommendations, become known in a specific niche, and your visibility – and business – will grow.

Get up to speed with LinkedIn

In this section, we will look at the steps you need to take to get up to speed with LinkedIn.

1 Create your profile.

2 Install applications.

3 Set up a LinkedIn Group.

4 Create an event.

5 Offer your expertise on LinkedIn Answers.

Create a profile

Think of your LinkedIn profile as selling copy. On Facebook you might talk about your hobbies or family in your personal profile. For LinkedIn, imagine you are updating your CV or résumé, or writing down your elevator pitch. Focus on your career history, education, achievements and what you can offer your contacts through your business. Add links to your websites so that people can find more information, and use plenty of keywords relevant to your industry, to boost your search results.

Build your network by importing your email contacts and searching for your business contacts. Look at your contacts' connections too for anyone you know. LinkedIn will also suggest people to connect to, based on your network, and is remarkably good at finding people for you – I'm still often surprised at how often LinkedIn correctly guesses 'people you may know'. It has better hit rate than Facebook, in my experience. But this is partly due to the restrictions built into the system. You are discouraged from connecting with just *anyone*.

❝ LinkedIn will also suggest people to connect to ❞

One part of your profile is 'Recommendations' – short testimonials written by contacts with whom you have done business. These are equivalent to references you may include with your CV or résumé, and don't be afraid to ask for them. There's even a form to make it easy for you. Go to the Profile Menu, choose Recommendations, then click the Request Recommendations tab. Or go direct to: www.linkedin.com/recRequests?cor=&trk=recppl_recsforme.

There's a standard message, which you can customise, and you can choose which position you want a recommendation for. This can also be a useful way to add testimonials to your website, since you can – and should – ask if you can quote from their recommendation on your website too.

figure 12.1 Request recommendations on LinkedIn

Install applications

LinkedIn now also has a range of apps to enhance your profile and increase your functionality. Although nothing like on the scale of Facebook (about a dozen so far, including Events and Tweets), they are more business-focused. Find these in the Application Directory via the **More**... drop-down menu. You will also see apps you have already installed in this menu.

figure 12.2 LinkedIn More... menu

Import your Twitter feed and blog (there is more information on this in the quick win section), and experiment with other apps that seem relevant to your business.

- **Polls** is is a market research tool that allows you to collect data from your connections for free, or target selected groups of people on LinkedIn based on industry, demographic, job title, etc., for a pay-per-response fee.

- **Reading List by Amazon** allows you to share what you're reading with other LinkedIn members by linking to books on Amazon.com.

- **SideShare** or **Google Presentation** – if you regularly run courses, give seminars or speak at conferences to people in your industry, consider uploading a sample presentation using one of these.

- **Company Buzz** tracks what's being said about your company on Twitter, blogs and elsewhere.

- **Box.net Files** allows file sharing with colleagues and specific contacts on LinkedIn.

- **My Travel**, powered by TripIt, alerts your network to where you'll be travelling. Useful for letting your contacts know when you'll be in the same city as them, or if you travel frequently to meet clients, to conferences, or to run seminars.

- **Huddle Workspaces** allows for private collaboration on projects with colleagues. Documents and spreadsheets can be co-edited with changes tracked.

■ **SAP Community Bio** is for those certified in SAP business software, and displays their credentials on their profiles.

■ **WordPress** and **Blog Link** – if you have a blog, pull your latest postings on to your profile with WordPress (for WordPress blogs), or Blog Link, which is powered by TypePad but works with any blog, and will pull in posts from multiple blogs.

■ **Events** displays events that you and your contacts plan to attend. You can also use it to create your own events, which we shall look at later in this chapter.

■ **Tweets** is one of the most useful apps, as it syncs with your Twitter account(s), and is a useful way to aggregate your updates and lessen the workload. Here's how:

Linking in with Twitter

Since 2009 LinkedIn has enabled you to link your Twitter account to your LinkedIn status update. Install the Tweets app, and configure the settings. You can choose Tweets from the More... drop-down menu, but

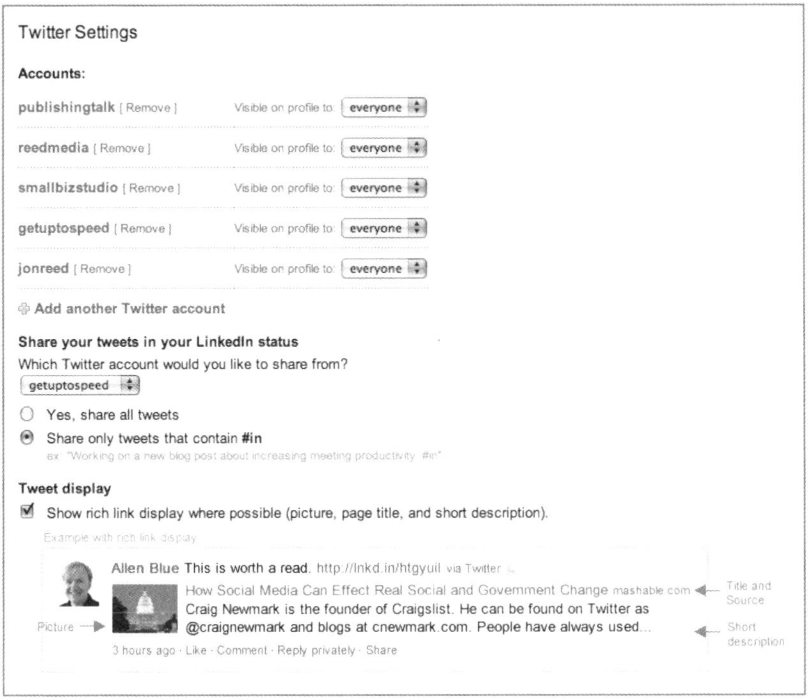

figure 12.3 LinkedIn Twitter settings

that will only allow you to adjust settings for the Twitter account that is linked to your updates.

If you have multiple Twitter accounts, click on **Settings** at the very top of the page, and then click on **Twitter Settings** – one of the options under **Profile Settings**. You will then be able to add several Twitter accounts, and choose which one you want to link to LinkedIn.

You can add as many Twitter accounts as you like. To add a new account, first make sure that you are logged in to the correct account in Twitter. Click Add another Twitter account, and you will see this screen pop-up:

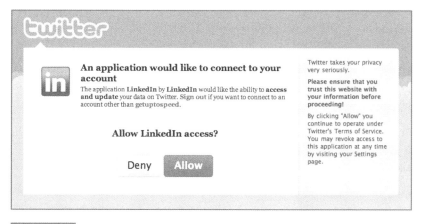

figure 12.4 Connect to Twitter

Click **Allow** – and you're done. If, like me, you have more than one Twitter account added, you need to choose which one you want to become your LinkedIn status. You can change this as often as you want – but you can only use one at a time. Choose one from the drop-down menu.

Your final option is to share all your tweets, or only those that contain the hashtag **#in** (**#li** also works). I recommend selective tweeting. Each social network you use is subtly different, is used for different purposes, and has a slightly different audience. Your LinkedIn contacts may be different people to your Facebook friends, for example, and be interested in different, more business-oriented information. Selective tweeting enables you to keep your updates relevant to your community.

Set up a LinkedIn group

LinkedIn Groups are communities of interest within the wider LinkedIn network. Many professional associations have LinkedIn Groups, which are worth joining and contributing to. But with over half a million LinkedIn Groups to choose from, there's bound to be several relevant to you.

You can also set up your own in your area of interest. I have a Publishing Talk LinkedIn Group that I use to promote the website and connect with publishing professionals around the world. I set this up partly because I knew many existing blog readers were already on LinkedIn, and it was a way of keeping in touch with them there as well as reaching out to new people. Plus I offer workshops to publishers, and people on LinkedIn tend to be interested in professional development.

You can also create subgroups. For example, there is an overall FT Prentice Hall LinkedIn Group, and this book has its own subgroup within it, which pulls in the RSS feed from the blog to the Discussions section.

You can create a group for your company, brand or website; or just set up a group in your topic area. If you do this, search existing groups first to see where the opportunities are to differentiate yourself.

One of the advantages of your own group is that it can help you grow your personal network within those niches that interest you most, since you can invite members from your group to become contacts. These are people that you might not have found by doing a search, but by creating a group they want to join, they have found you.

LinkedIn is a bit strict about who you can invite to join your contacts – it should be people you know or have done business with. However, you can also invite people who are fellow members of a LinkedIn group.

You should always try to use a more personalised invitation than the default 'I'd like to add you to my professional network on LinkedIn' message!

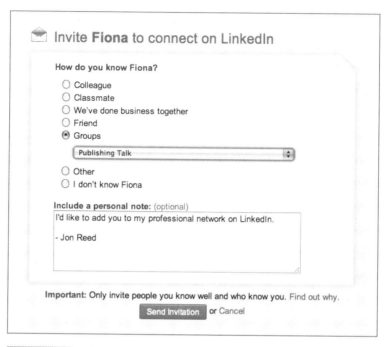

figure 12.5 Invite people to connect on LinkedIn

To create your LinkedIn Group, go to the Groups tab, click Create a Group and fill in the details.

figure 12.6 LinkedIn groups tab

Make sure you upload a logo – once people start joining, this 'badge' will show up on their profile, and if your group looks interesting to their contacts, they may click on it and join too. Add a description with plenty of keywords, include your website, and choose a group type. This will most likely be 'Networking Group' or 'Professional Group'.

You have the option of choosing either:

- ◼ **Open Access**: Any LinkedIn member may join this group without requiring approval from a manager.
- ◼ **Request to Join**: Users must request to join this group and be approved by a manager.

You should always choose the former to reduce any barriers to building up your membership.

Once you have your group set up, you'll need to add content to it to keep people interested. Group members can start discussions, add news, and post job ads in your group (subject to the settings you choose), but you need to do some of the work too. Thing you can add are:

- ◼ **Discussions** – start a discussion topic, or simply post a message to the Discussion area. As administrator, you can also make this a 'featured' item that appears at the top of the list.
- ◼ **Links** – attatch links to Discussions, with a short description. One of the most useful options here is to automatically pull in your latest blog posts (see quick win).
- ◼ **Job Ads** – your group comes with a jobs board.

Add at least some content before inviting your contacts – even if it is just a welcome message. And don't invite everyone – just those who you think will be interested. Promote your group as you would with a Facebook group or any new social media channel you start using: put it in your email signature, include a prominent link on your website, write a blog post about it, mention it in your next email newsletter, tweet about it, etc.

One of the benefits of groups – whether your own or someone else's that you post to – is that the items you submit to them are included in digest emails to group members who accept notifications from the group. With your own group, you can also send a message to all the members of your group, which sends an email as well as posting to the Discussion area. Use this sparingly (LinkedIn will only allow one of these per week) and think carefully about your message content, as you would with any other mass mailing. Because these emails come from linkedin.com, they have a high deliverability – they're less likely to get caught in spam filters.

quick win

Make your latest blog posts your group discussions

Keeping your LinkedIn group fresh is important, since this is a way to deliver useful content to your target market. To save you having to update your group's discussions all the time, pull in the RSS feed from your blog.

▪ Go to the **Manage** tab of your group.

▪ Click on **Manage news feeds**.

▪ Add your RSS URL, or simply your web address, and you're done.

You can even add several RSS feeds. And all your discussions – including your latest blog postings – get emailed to your members from LinkedIn, without you even having to visit LinkedIn to maintain your group.

figure 12.7 Manage news feeds in LinkedIn groups

Create a LinkedIn event

Go to the 'More...' tab at the top of your screen, and choose Events.

Click on the **Add an Event** tab, and enter your event details. You can either click on the **Add more details** link at the bottom to add a blurb, keywords, a category and more for your event – or edit these in afterwards.

Your event is now live, and will appear in your news feed for all your contacts to see. You also have the option to invite specific people from your network, or promote your event with an ad.

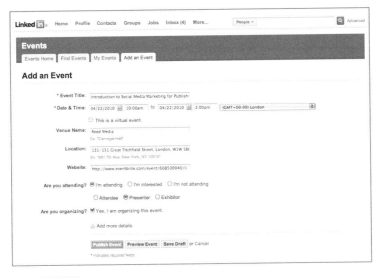

figure 12.8   Create a LinkedIn event

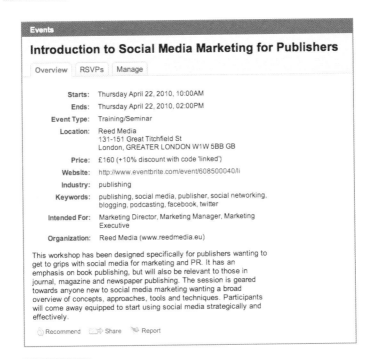

figure 12.9   LinkedIn event

Offer your expertise on LinkedIn answers

The other powerful tool available to you on LinkedIn is Answers. You can ask questions of the LinkedIn network, or you can answer questions that others have asked – which can be great way to promote your expertise, build connections and drive people to your website.

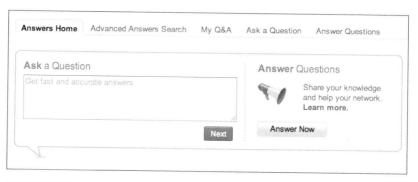

figure 12.10 LinkedIn answers

Questions are categorised into a range of business-oriented categories and subcategories. You can browse these for the latest questions in your field, or use the Advanced Search. Is your specialism intellectual property law? There's a subcategory for that:

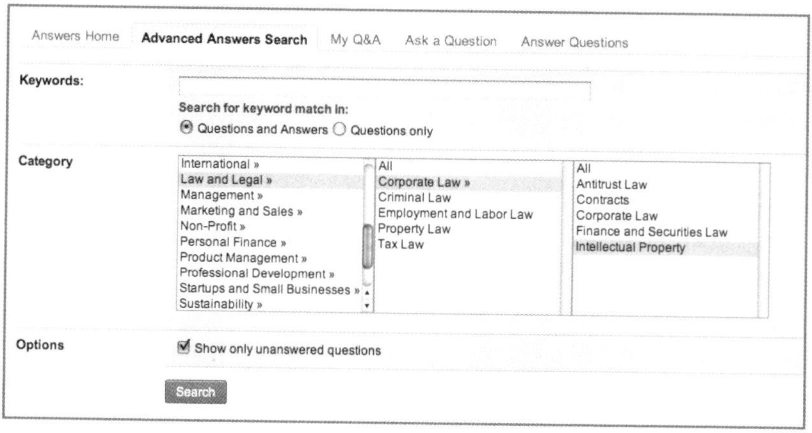

figure 12.11 Advanced answers search

On the results page for your category search you can browse all questions or just those that are still open by using the navigation tabs. You can also further refine your search using keywords, and tick the **show only unanswered questions** if you want to be the first to offer an answer.

figure 12.12   Search results for LinkedIn questions by category

Once you find a question you can answer helpfully and well, fill in your response. This will be visible to all LinkedIn users. If you've previously written a blog post about the topic, include that in the Web Resources field. Don't include your own web address here, or elsewhere in your answer – the focus must be on providing useful information, and your name and job role will show up anyway.

If you know someone else who is even better placed to answer the question, click the Suggest Experts button. This helps the questioner, and helps you build a connection with the expert you suggest.

The more you participate in LinkedIn Answers, the more authority, trust and respect you will build. People who ask questions on LinkedIn can choose which answer they think was the best – so your focus should be on trying to provide the best answers in your chosen category. LinkedIn highlights the areas in which you've submitted the best answers in your profile and in the box with your name and position that shows up next to your answers.

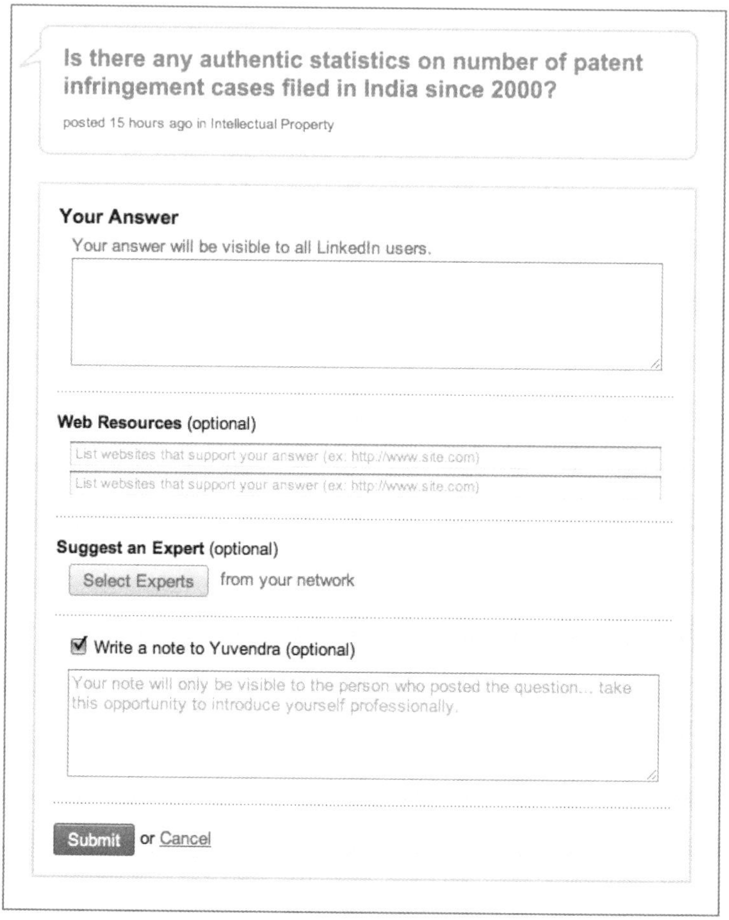

Is there any authentic statistics on number of patent infringement cases filed in India since 2000?

posted 15 hours ago in Intellectual Property

Your Answer
Your answer will be visible to all LinkedIn users.

Web Resources (optional)

List websites that support your answer (ex: http://www.site.com)

List websites that support your answer (ex: http://www.site.com)

Suggest an Expert (optional)

Select Experts   from your network

☑ Write a note to Yuvendra (optional)

Your note will only be visible to the person who posted the question... take this opportunity to introduce yourself professionally.

Submit or Cancel

figure 12.13 Submitting a LinkedIn answer

Manage the workload

Now that LinkedIn has apps, it is possible to aggregate some of your other social media using the WordPress, Blog Link and Tweets apps. That way you can keep the content on your LinkedIn profile fresh, without logging in every day.

Keeping your LinkedIn group fresh is even more important, since this is a way to deliver useful content to your target market, and from a highly deliverable LinkedIn email address too. To save you having to update your group's news items all the time, pull in the RSS feed from your blog.

To spread the workload of managing your group, you can promote up to nine members to manager status, and up to 50 to moderator. Click on the Manage tab, and select the links from the left-hand menu.

Finally, don't forget to keep your LinkedIn status updates fresh. If you use www.tweetdeck.com to manage your Twitter accounts and Facebook or MySpace statuses, you can now also use this to update LinkedIn from the same interface. You can also automatically pull in your tweets to your LinkedIn status, but I'd recommend choosing the selective tweets option (only pulling in tweets ending #in) to keep the noise down.

> **❝ don't forget to keep your LinkedIn status updates fresh ❞**

Measure your results

The number of contacts in your network is one measure, if a blunt one, of your success on LinkedIn. But it is the quality of those connections rather than the numbers that are important. Other metrics you should be looking to boost are:

- your Group members, since this can be a key opted-in mailing list for you on LinkedIn
- your ratings in LinkedIn Answers
- responses to your events.

Use tracking links and discount codes to measure the effectiveness of LinkedIn for selling event registrations. Use your web-stats package to track the traffic coming to your site from LinkedIn, and/or use unique URLs to measure its effectiveness in driving people to your site.

Take action

▪ **Set up** an account at at www.linkedin.com.

▪ **Create** a profile. Keep it business-focused, include a link to your business, and solicit recommendations.

▪ **Add** connections, and find more by searching.

▪ **Join** groups relevant to your business.

▪ **Start** your own group, and pull your blog into its Discussions section.

▪ **Create** a LinkedIn event if you run events for business professionals.

▪ **Sync** with your Twitter account to reduce the amount of updates you need to do – but tweet selectively using the #in tag.

▪ **Find** some questions to answer and share your expertise.

Tap into Twitter

How to use the power of the real-time web to build a following

What are you doing right now? How about now? Now? That's quite annoying, isn't it? But it's a question answered millions of times a day by over 75 million users of Twitter, the world's fastest growing social network. For those who haven't yet dipped a toe in the collective stream of consciousness that is the Twitterverse, it seems a bit of a mad idea. Much maligned by those who see only the egocentric inanity of it, there is far more to Twitter than 'having a cup of tea' style status updates. It is used in a variety of creative ways by both individuals and businesses, to make connections, build a loyal following, create a useful news feed, and share links to articles, images, audio and video.

What is Twitter?

If you're familiar with Facebook, Twitter is basically just the status update part of Facebook. It's a short update (or 'tweet') that tells the world what you're up to, or indeed any message, as often as you like, in 140 characters or less. Twitter is described as a 'microblogging' site, which suggests it is a content tool, made up of very short blog posts. While true, the way in which Twitter is now used is much more social, which makes me think of it as more of a social network, and therefore an outreach tool. The truth lies somewhere in between.

> **Twitter is basically just the status update part of Facebook**

Why does Twitter work for business?

The value of Twitter is in its ability to reach a vast yet niche audience of people who are interested in what you have to say. You can build a following as an authentic, trusted voice in your field. Its real-time 'breaking news' aspect, plus its widespread use on mobile devices, makes it a medium for providing valuable information for your community of interest where and when they want it. You can let people know what is going on right now, tweet breaking news, plus more commercial messages such as time-limited discounts and special offers.

Twitter becomes more or less useful depending on who you follow. For example, I follow a number of other social media enthusiasts on Twitter. At any one time, they are attending international conferences and live-tweeting from them, discussing latest trends and developments in the field, and sharing links. It helps me keep current. If you can provide similarly useful information to your community, you will build a loyal following.

> ❝ Twitter becomes more or less useful depending on who you follow ❞

Twitter's usefulness is similar to building an email list – and it is an opt-in list, since people have sought you out and chosen to follow you for the valuable, interesting content you provide. This may sometimes include news of your latest products, special offers, and relevant links to your blog or website.

Twitter in action

Hippo (www.hippofighthunger.com)

In 2009, Indian food and beverage company Parle Agro launched a snack food brand called 'Hippo'. Working with Creativeland Asia, they experimented with Twitter to crowdsource a solution to a problem: how to maintain retail inventory in a country the size of India.

The character of Hippo has been developed via a microsite (www.hippofighthunger.com), and in 2010 Hippo started tweeting from @HelloMeHippo and blogging at http://hippofighthunger.blogspot.com.

Competitions and giveaways are promoted via Twitter, and a high level of engagement with customers is achieved through replies and retweets, and Hippo's unique take on the world, including current events. But the greatest business benefit is Hippo's request that people tweet him whenever they couldn't find Hippo in stores.

Home Profile Find People Settings Help Sign out

Hippo say please, please help Hippo fight hunger by telling Hippo where Hippo not available. Shop name, Area name, surname any detail do.

10:11 AM May 6th via web

Reply   Retweet

HelloMeHippo
Hippo

figure 13.1 @HelloMeHippo ask for help

This has enabled Parle Agro to restock stores within hours, and identify new markets. At zero cost, Hippo receives tweets from people in 25 cities equivalent to almost half its sales force. By using the real-time web to match sales with demand more efficiently, and increase sales by 76 per cent in the first few months after launch[6].

Get the idea: Use the size and real-time nature of Twitter, plus tweeters' willingness to help, to crowdsource a business function. And when it comes to engaging your audience, there's no reason why your Twitter account can't be a character tied strongly to your brand.

Get up to speed with Twitter

In this chapter we'll look at the essential steps you need to take to use Twitter effectively for your business.

1 Create your Twitter account.

2 Familiarise yourself with Twitter.

3 Get tweeting!

4 Build your followers.

6 http://www.campaignasia.com/Article/214608,case-study-parle-agros-hippo-turns-to-twitter-to-track-inventory-and-replenish-stocks.aspx

Create your Twitter account

You can start to get a feel for Twitter at http://twitter.com without even creating an account. You can see what the current 'trending topics' are (i.e. what people are tweeting about most often), and do a search yourself. But the best way to learn about the possibilities is to sign up and start tweeting.

1 **Register an account at** http://twitter.com/signup. You can change your 'Full name', password and email later if you want – but think carefully about the username you choose, since this will appear in the URL (e.g. http://twitter.com/jonreed). It's a bit like registering a web address. You can also change this later, but you're unlikely to want to once you build up a following. You can create a personal account, a business account, or both.

2 **Upload a profile picture.** The most essential graphical element is your profile picture. You must have one of these. If you stick with the default Twitter bird icon, you will not be taken seriously on Twitter, and it will be hard to attract followers. There is evidence to suggest that people like to see a person rather than a company logo, but it's really up to you.

3 **Add a biography.** You can also include a short (160 character) description, or biography. You might choose to make this a personal biography, or a description of your business. You can also keep changing this if you want, perhaps to focus on a particular project, product, service or offer.

4 **Include your web address.** This appears prominently on your profile page. Think carefully about where you want to link to, and again you can change this whenever you want. You will probably want to link to the home page of your business site, but you may also want to link to your blog, or to a special offer, or a newly launched product or service. Many people will click on this link to see who is behind the Twitter profile, so use it wisely.

5 **Do NOT protect your updates.** There is an option for you to pre-approve your followers, by selecting 'protect my updates'. Don't do this unless you want to be invisible on Twitter.

6 **Customise your background.** It is fairly easy to customise your colour scheme: just go to **Settings**, **Design** and **Change design colors** (http://twitter.com/settings/design). You should choose

colours that match your branding. But you can also click on **Change background image** from this screen and include a customised, branded background. There are advantages to doing this, including the opportunity to add a graphical sidebar that contains more information about your business. There is further information on how to do this at www.getuptospeed.biz/twitterback. But don't worry if you don't have a customised background, at least to start with – a lot of people will never see your Twitter page anyway, since they'll follow your tweets on their own timeline, or via a smartphone or desktop application such as www.tweetdeck.com.

Familiarise yourself with Twitter

Finding your way around

Now, get to know the different elements of your Twitter page. This is the Profile page for this book's Twitter account, which is what you'll see if you go to http://twitter.com/getuptospeed:

figure 13.2 Twitter profile page

Actually, that's what I see when I visit @getuptospeed when logged into my personal account as @jonreed. There's a big tick and 'Following' to show I'm following this Twitter account. If I wasn't, there would be a 'Follow' button to click. On the right-hand column you'll see there's a link to the website for this book, a short bio, and you can click to see who I'm following, who is following me and who has listed me. Further down, there is a list called 'casestudies', which displays as @getuptospeed/casestudies, which visitors can view and follow if they wish. More on lists later.

If you hover over an individual tweet, it appears shaded and displays a few more options.

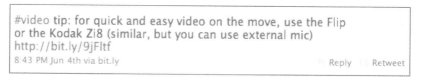

#video tip: for quick and easy video on the move, use the Flip or the Kodak Zi8 (similar, but you can use external mic) http://bit.ly/9jFltf
8:43 PM Jun 4th via bit.ly   Reply   Retweet

figure 13.3 Additional options for individual tweets

- Click the **star icon** to 'favourite' a tweet. Other people can see your favourites by clicking on the sidebar link, so choose these carefully. I tend to favourite any testimonials on my business accounts, and also post these on my websites.
- Click **Reply** to send a public @ reply (a tweet that starts: '@getuptospeed').
- Click **Retweet** to pass on the tweet to your followers. You will be asked to confirm that you really want to do this.

#video tip: for quick and easy video on the move, use the Flip or the Kodak Zi8 (similar, but you can use external mic) http://bit.ly/9jFltf
8:43 PM Jun 4th via bit.ly   Reply ↻ Retweet

#websites tip: Be shallow. Keep shallow–i.e. not too many leve content.
7:55 PM Jun 3rd via TweetDeck

Retweet to your followers?   **Yes**

figure 13.4 Retweet button

And then the tweet will appear with a retweet icon in front of it, on both
its own and your Twitter page.

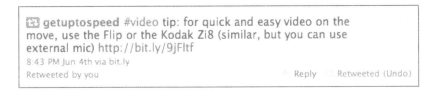

> **ᘳ getuptospeed** #video tip: for quick and easy video on the
> move, use the Flip or the Kodak Zi8 (similar, but you can use
> external mic) http://bit.ly/9jFltf
> 8:43 PM Jun 4th via bit.ly
> Retweeted by you   Reply   Retweeted (Undo)

figure 13.5 A retweeted tweet

If I log into Twitter as @getuptospeed, I see a different home page – one
made up of a timeline of all the people I follow:

figure 13.6 Twitter home page

I can still see the other view of my own tweets by clicking on Profile. But on this home page, I see a different right-hand sidebar, including links to:

▪ **@getuptospeed** – i.e. any tweets that include '@getuptospeed'. These tweets are considered replies if they start with @getuptospeed, and mentions if they include it elsewhere within the tweet.

▪ **Direct Messages** – these are private messages that only I can see, as opposed to an @ reply, which is in public.

▪ **Favorites** – any tweets I have favourited.

▪ **Retweets** – I can see any tweets that have been retweeted by people I follow; tweets that I have retweeted; and all my tweets that have been retweeted by others.

figure 13.7 Keeping track of retweets

Further down the sidebar is a list of the top ten trending topics – the most commonly used words, phrases used on Twitter right now in the UK. You can choose which region to show, or select Worldwide.

Twitter lists

One of the newer developments with Twitter is Twitter lists. Anyone can add other Twitter users to a list, and call it whatever they want. Just click the Lists button you'll see at the top of everyone's Twitter page, and tick any existing lists you have, or create a new one.

What is the advantage of this? Once you are following a lot of people, creating discrete lists will enable you to create a subset of followers, a different timeline to view, to filter out the noise. And it can create a useful list of people for others to follow too – in this case, the businesses who are mentioned in this book.

figure 13.8 Adding people to Twitter lists

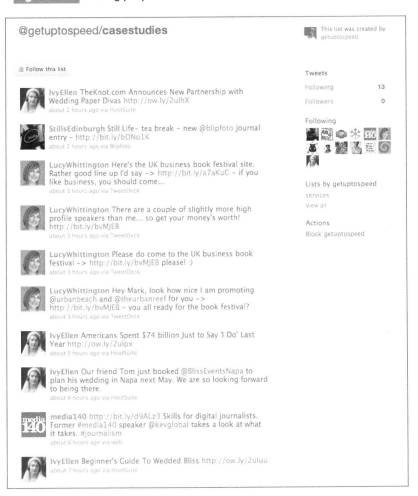

figure 13.9 A Twitter list

quick win

Create a Twitter list widget

Go a stage further and import a Twitter list into your blog or website using the Twitter list widget. I do this with my Reed Media clients by adding a Twitter list widget that displays the list I've created at @reedmedia/clients to the 'Clients' page of my website, showing what they are tweeting in real time. Do something similar to give your clients more prominence on your website, or include a list of all your colleagues who are on Twitter.

■ Go to http://twitter.com/goodies/widget_list.

■ Your username will be included by default – but you can even create a list widget from someone else's list if you want, so long as they have made it public. Once you have the Twitter username you want to use, select the list you want from the drop-down menu.

■ Enter whatever title and caption you want. You'll see a preview on the right-hand side.

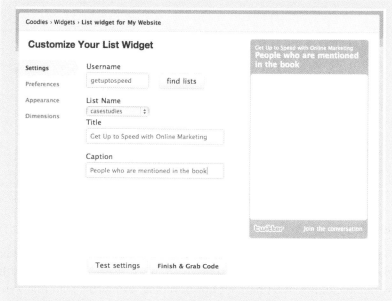

figure 13.10 Customise your Twitter list widget

▪ Click the **Preferences, Appearance** and **Dimensions** links on the left-hand side to customise further.

▪ Click **Test settings** to see your tweets appear.

▪ Click **Finish & Grab Code**.

▪ Add the code to your blog or website. You will only need to do this once, since whenever you add a new person to your Twitter list, they will automatically show up in your widget too.

figure 13.11 Preview your list widget and grab the code

Get Tweeting

You can tweet in the 'traditional' way, to post updates about whatever you're doing this minute. But there is so much more you can do with Twitter, including tweeting your business blog, using the 'real-time web' aspect of it to tweet latest news and time-limited discount codes, and – especially – to create a useful news feed for your community of interest. This will make them want to follow you, build an opted-in mailing list for you, and draw them on to your website. As with any form of social media, it's the usefulness of your content that will attract followers.

Here are my top 10 ways to make the most of Twitter.

1. Create a valuable news service If you want people to follow you, create a useful feed to follow. That may be announcements, news and links about your industry or field, and can help position you as an expert. It might be original tips you write yourself. A daily tip on your area of expertise can be a powerful way to build a following. But just keeping an eye on tweets in your area of interest and retweeting them is in itself useful, and a low-maintenance way to keep your tweets regular.

2. Include relevant links Tweets are most useful when they include a *relevant* link to something useful or interesting. This may be a blog post, a news item, a press release, a YouTube video – almost anything. And to make sure you don't take up too much valuable space in your allocated 140 characters, use a free URL shortening service such as http://tinyurl.com, http://bit.ly, http://snipurl.com or http://is.gd. My favourite is http://bit.ly (pronounced 'Bitly'), because you can use it with multiple Twitter accounts, and it comes with plenty of analytics that can give you an insight into how many people are clicking on your links.

figure 13.12 Bit.ly

You can also add the 'shorten with bit.ly' toolbar to your browser: simply click on **Tools**, then drag the **Shorten with bit.ly** link to your browser's toolbar. Go to a web page you want to share on Twitter, click the **Shorten with bit.ly** button that now appears on your toolbar, and tweet it with your message to whichever Twitter account(s) you want.

Once you start including links in your tweets, they become more useful to your followers, and your Twitter feed becomes full of information that your community will value.

3. Tweet your blog The best way of generating web traffic based on relevant, contextual links is to tweet your blog. You can set up an account with www.twitterfeed.com to link any blog to a Twitter account. Whenever you publish a new post, it will automatically tweet to your account with a link back to your blog post. Remember to include your own tweets as well as simply dumping links to your blog, to maintain engagement with your audience and increase your followers. You might consider asking a question relevant to a blog post that has recently tweeted.

4. Link to pictures, audio and video You can enhance your content by including links to the three other Internet content types: images, video and audio. Use http://twitpic.com, http://tweetphoto.com or http://yfrog.com to upload a picture with your tweet. Use www.twitvid.com or www.twiddeo.com to upload video. Tweet audio with http://audioboo.fm, such as quick client testimonials, short interviews at trade shows, or simply to speak directly to your customers.

5. Use Twitter as a search engine Twitter can be a valuable source of market intelligence when used as a 'listening tool' to find out what people are saying about you, or your business sector. Twitter has a powerful, integrated search function in the sidebar on your page. You can also go to http://search.twitter.com. Both of these display the latest 'trending topics'. Most importantly, you can use it to find and follow people whose tweets include your keywords – search terms that are relevant to the community you're trying to reach.

6. Special offers and freebies You can encourage followers by offering something for free to new followers – such as an e-book. Explain the offer in your biography or graphical sidebar, as well as on your website and anywhere else you want to attract people who are not yet on Twitter. You can set up an automatic welcome DM to new followers at www.tweetlater.com – and include a link to the download. I'm not a fan of automatic DMs, even when you're giving something away – but not everyone objects. Another way to organise a giveaway is to use http://twiveaway.com to run a contest. Ask people to retweet a specific message over a given time period, and then pull, say, six names out of a hat to receive a free gift, all managed for you by Twiveaway. Another approach is to tweet regular time-limited discount codes – something that South African T-shirt store Spring Leap (@Springleap) have used successfully. For people who are interested in their products, it pays to follow them on Twitter since they'll have access to discounts. They also engage their community with competitions.

figure 13.13 @Springleap offer a time-limited discount

7. Organise a tweet-up Twitterers don't just sit in front of their computer screens all day – they like to get together at real-life meet-ups, or 'tweet-ups'. If you have a loyal following of people who are united by a common interest, consider organising a get-together. It doesn't have to be a big event – a few drinks in a bar after work would do. You could provide free drinks by sponsoring the event yourself, or even finding an external sponsor to put a tab behind the bar. And it's very easy to organise through Twitter using http://twtvite.com. If your business serves a local community, you might consider organising and sponsoring a local tweet-up. Twestival (http://twestival.com) has raised half a million dollars for charity primarily through local tweet-ups throughout the world. The focus doesn't have to be purely social: you could also arrange a guest speaker, or speak yourself, on the topic of interest to your community. You might even consider charging for events that provide significant value to your followers.

> **❝ Twitterers like to get together at real-life meet-ups, or 'tweet-ups' ❞**

8. Conduct market research Social media enables you to stay close to your community, and this is useful for ad hoc market research. Ask your community what they think about a new product, service or website. Create an online survey using www.surveymonkey.com and promote it via Twitter, do a poll with http://twtpoll.com, or simply ask a question with a tweet. When Rude Health Cereals owner Camilla Barnard (@rudehealth) wants some feedback on a new idea for a porridge flavour, she simply asks. And because it's not a focus group where people feel worried to speak up, she gets direct and honest feedback.

9. Ask for help People are very willing to help out on Twitter. I offer advice where I can, but I also ask for it. Sometimes I ask for geek help such as 'Do you know of a WordPress plugin that does X?' But because publishers and authors are also part of my community of interest, I also follow a lot of writers. A couple of months ago I tweeted 'I want to go away for a week to focus on writing. Any suggestions?' I had several suggestions within the hour, including from a writer friend called Katharine (@kreeve), who I only know from Twitter: '@jonreed – suggest Alf Rescos in Dartmouth – top flat – excellent breakfasts and coffee; big table, mini kitchen, overlooking sea and Dart'. And that is exactly where I am writing from – somewhere I would never have discovered without Twitter!

10. Improve customer service Use the real-time web to respond to customers and even to take orders. Small, independent Houston-based coffee shop CoffeeGroundz (@CoffeeGroundz) is credited with taking the first 'to-go' order on Twitter, from one of their regular customers, Sean Stoner (@maslowbeer). Because general manager J.R. Cohen is an avid tweeter, he quickly replied and this started a trend: 'to-go' orders, table reservations and event bookings are now regularly taken from all their followers via Direct Message (DM). Together with free wi-fi, this has made the coffee shop a firm favourite of the local Twitterati, as well as gaining the business wider publicity.

Build your followers

Now that you're on Twitter with a nice branded profile, tweeting appropriately and engagingly and following key people in your community, it's time to build your followers. Why do you want to do this? Because building followers on Twitter is like building up your email list. Once you have a sizable list, you can announce your latest product, service or event – so long as it is genuinely of interest to your followers and you're not doing a hard sell. Like an email list, you don't want people on there who are not interested in what you're offering. You don't want to randomly broadcast a wasted marketing message – you want to engage your fan base of followers who are actually interested in what you do.

The big secret is simply: *follow more people*. About half will follow you back. OK, there is a bit more to it, and a few caveats. Here is my Five-Point Exploding Twitter Technique, for significantly increasing your followers while maintaining their value.

1. Only follow people who are in your community of interest Follow people who are likely to be interested in you and follow you back. Where do you find them? One way is to do a keyword search for people who are tweeting about your topic, or look at who is tweeting from a conference within your industry by following the hashtag. A more efficient way is to find people like yourself, who are tweeting in your subject area – and follow their followers. Their followers are also likely to be interested in your tweets, if they're already following someone who is your 'competition' in the Twitterverse. To find these people, look at some of the Twitter directories that sort people according to industry or topic, such as www.wefollow. com or www.twellow.com.

2. Stay within the Twitter follow limit There is a limit – you can't just follow everyone. Twitter will stop you from following any new people once you hit the limit. However, that limit increases the more followers you have. Anyone can follow 2,000 people. After that, you can follow 10 per cent more people than are following you. So, if you have 5,000 followers, you can follow 5,500 people.

3. Unfollow people who don't follow you back Does that seem harsh? Not really. If people don't follow you back, they're clearly not that interested in what you have to say. Just like you don't want random, uninterested, disengaged people clogging up your email list, you don't want uninterested people taking up valuable space in your allowance of people you can follow. In this way you can free up space for new people to follow. You can find those people who you follow but who don't follow you by using http://friendorfollow.com.

4. Create content that people actually want to read Finding followers is easy. Keeping them is harder. In the same way people can stop subscribing to your email newsletters, they can stop following you on Twitter. If you stay focused on engaging your followers with useful, interesting, regular content, you will not only keep your followers but also attract new ones. There's no real substitute for creating a useful news service.

5. Create community by using hashtags (#), retweets (RT) and replies (@) By using Twitter in a social way, rather than treating it as a one-way broadcast medium, you increase the interest and value in your tweets, which will make you more interesting to follow. Hashtags are keywords that start with the # symbol and become hotlinks to a timeline of everyone tweeting with that hashtag in their tweets. They are popular at conferences, where delegates frequently tweet what is going on, with the hashtag (e.g. #lbf10 for the London Book Fair 2010). That means that everyone can follow what is going on – whether they are at the conference or not. Hashtags will also make you more visible to people doing keyword searches using hashtags. Do this authentically though – don't hijack a trending topic! Find out more about hashtags at www.getuptospeed.biz/hashtags.

This can be a bit time-consuming. But by following this strategy you can incrementally increase your followers to very high levels in a relatively short space of time. What's more, the people on the list you're building are all interested in what you have to say – and they have *chosen* to follow you! Even if you followed them first, the choice to follow you back is theirs, so this is an opted-in mailing list of people in your community of interest.

As your list of followers grows, your 10 per cent allowance grows with it. And having a high number of followers also makes you more visible on Twitter, since more people are likely to retweet your posts, and you appear higher up in your sector in the Twitter directories. This means you may only need to actively increase your followers when you first start using Twitter since, once you reach a critical mass of followers, your Twitter success will build on itself.

❝ having a high number of followers also makes you more visible on Twitter ❞

Manage the workload

So how will you find time for all those updates? Like other forms of social media, the key is to integrate it into your working life.

On your desktop There are also various desktop widgets and applications you can download which provide a running 'tick' of your friends' tweets in real time on your desktop. TweetDeck (www.tweetdeck.com) is particularly useful if you have multiple Twitter accounts, since you can manage and update all of them – plus Facebook, MySpace and LinkedIn – from a single browser interface. You can set up as different columns for each account. Mine include: a column showing all the people I follow on my personal @jonreed account; a column showing replies from all my Twitter accounts, so that I can respond to anything I need to; and a column displaying the results of a Twitter search for the keyword 'publishing', which enables me to keep an eye on any interesting tweets and links that might be interesting to my @publishingtalk followers. I can then retweet them with a couple of clicks – it takes no time at all. You can use this feature to monitor keywords or hashtags, for example if you're following the action at a conference via Twitter.

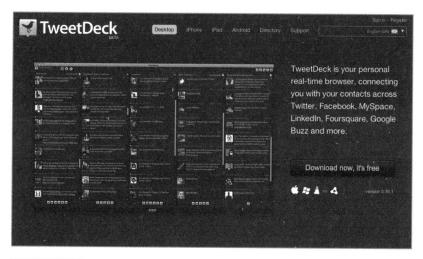

figure 13.14 TweetDeck

On the move If you have an iPhone, you can download one of several apps, including Twitterific, Tweetie, Echofon and TweetDeck. These also integrate automatically with Twitpic or Tweetphoto, so you can take a photo with your phone and upload it with your tweet. You can also do all this via mobile Internet. And if you don't have a smartphone, you can simply text your tweet to a specific number you can find in your account settings. Tweeting is a great thing to do whenever you have a minute of dead time: waiting for a client to arrive, on the train, waiting for the bus, etc.

Share the workload The flipside of managing multiple Twitter accounts with TweetDeck is to have several people managing one Twitter account. Use Cotweet for this (www.cotweet.com), which is used by many businesses. You can also assign updates to colleagues for follow-up and 'on duty' notifications.

Schedule Write your tweets in advance, and schedule them over time with http://hootsuite.com, which also has a wealth of other tools to manage your tweets and analyse your impact. You can also schedule tweets for future release using TweetDeck.

Aggregate Other ways include using an aggregator like www.ping.fm, from where you can write status updates and have them sent where you wish, including Twitter and Facebook. Use FriendFeed to aggregate all your social media, including Twitter accounts, blog feeds, Flickr photos, YouTube videos and many many more.

Integrate Once you have FriendFeed set up, use the Facebook FriendFeed app to pull all those updates back into your Facebook profile. You can also have your tweet automatically become your Facebook status update, again reducing the need to be in two places at once. You can use the Twitter app in Facebook to do this; or, if you want to be selective about which tweets become Facebook status updates and manage multiple Twitter accounts and multiple Facebook pages, use the Selective Tweet Status app in Facebook (http://apps.facebook.com/selectivetwitter). Automatically have your new blog posts tweet to your account, using www.twitterfeed.com.

❝ go a stage further and reimport your latest tweets into your website ❞

You should, of course, link to your Twitter account from your website or blog. But you can go a stage further than this and reimport your latest tweets into your website using a widget. You can set up and customise widgets at http://twitter.com/goodies/widgets. If you use a WordPress blog, you can also pull your tweets into your blog using one of many plugins available, such as Twitter Tools (www.alexking.org/projects/wordpress).

Measure your results

Finally, has it all been worth it? How do you know if your Twitter strategy is a success? Because Twitter make their programming interface open to anyone, there is a vast amount of third-party tools out there to help you.

1　**Count the numbers.** How many followers do you have? You can track the trend over time using www.twittercounter.com. You can look up anyone's follower stats – not just your own – and show off your own web stats with a TwitterCounter badge on your website.

publishingtalk twitter statistics Update stats now :

Publishing Talk | http://www.publishingtalk.eu
Bio: The online community for authors and publishers interested in social media, digital, and the future of the publishing industry. Run by @jonreed.

Followers | Following | Tweets | Mixed

Graph size: Weekly **Monthly** 3-Monthly

Tomorrow
59,544 (+202)

59,342
Followers
+222 yesterday
+181 on average

27,424
Following
+227 yesterday
+201 on average

1,118
Tweets
+0 yesterday
+2 on average

#3,036
Twitter rank
3,051
yesterday

New! Predictions
Find out how your Twitter account will grow over time. Drag the slider and Tweet your followers prediction!

62,056 followers
in **15** days

335 days to reach
120,000 followers

figure 13.15 Twitter counter statistics

2 **Find out more about your followers.** www.twitteranalyzer.com is a useful tool that will give you lots of analytics, including where your followers are geographically. This is useful for deciding, say, which currency to price your products in, and when to tweet based on time zone. For example, I know that about 50 per cent of my @publishingtalk followers are in the USA – so there's little point in me tweeting before midday in the UK, since half my followers haven't woken up yet.

3 **Measure engagement.** The amount of retweets and replies you get will give you a clue. Like a blog, you could work out a conversational index based on your number of @replies divided by updates. You could

also use a sophisticated tool from TweetMeme called TweetMeme Analytics (http://tweetmeme.com/about/analytics) which gives you data on click-throughs, retweets, user demographics, most influential users and even the path through Twitter that your retweets take.

4 **Analyse your web stats.** The amount of traffic that comes to your website from Twitter, can be gleaned from a web-stats package that includes Twitter as a traffic source. I use Clicky for this (www.getclicky.com).

5 **Unique URLs.** If you use unique landing pages, you can be even more forensic about who is taking action as a result of your tweets. You can use one for your main URL on your profile – that will tell you how many people are clicking through to your website from your profile page. Or if you are tweeting a call to action, such as announcing a new product, inviting people to download a white paper, or promoting a special offer, you may want to use a unique landing page in your tweet too. You probably won't want to do this too often, since each one will take a little while to set up; but it will give you some very accurate stats about how many people are taking action in response to a specific tweet.

6 **Look up your ranking.** Use services like www.twitterrank.com and www.twittergrader.com to see where you rank, and look yourself up in directories such as www.wefollow.com.

Take action

■ **Set up** your Twitter account.

■ **Customise** your page with a profile picture and a background.

■ **Follow** people in your community of interest.

■ **Link** to your blog.

■ **Provide** a useful news service.

■ **Manage** the workload with www.tweetdeck.com.

■ **Tweet**, retweet, and repeat!.

14

Jack into the Matrix

How to make real money in virtual worlds

V irtual worlds, such as Second Life (http://secondlife.com), have the appearance of video games yet the functionality of social networks. They are harder to use than social networks, because you have to learn the interface first; and the hype and publicity surrounding them a few years back has now died down; but they should be treated like any other online social space: if your market spends time there, so should you.

What are virtual worlds?

Virtual worlds look like video games – but aren't. The 'characters' are in fact avatars – virtual representations of real people, behind their keyboards, all over the world.

Virtual worlds include World of Warcraft, Club Penguin (www.club penguin.com – owned by Disney and aimed at children), Entropia Universe (www.entropiauniverse.com) and Second Life (http://secondlife.com). It is even possible to create your own virtual world with an application called Unity (http://unity3d.com).

Launched in 2003 by Linden Labs, Second Life is by far the largest virtual world, with 18 million registered accounts as of January 2010 – although reliable figures for active residents are hard to come by. Because of its size, its proven business models and its real economy, Second Life is the virtual world most suited to promoting your business, and the one that I will therefore mostly focus on in this chapter.

" Second Life is the virtual world most suited to promoting your business "

Second Life (SL) has many of the same features as the real world – shops, universities, museums, nightclubs, even government departments. Sweden has an embassy there, and the UK National Health Service has a virtual outpost run jointly with Imperial College London. Many universities have virtual campuses in SL, including Harvard, MIT, Ohio University, The Open University, and the London School of Journalism, who require their students to attend at least one lecture in SL. Education is one area where Second Life seems to be finding its niche.

Virtual worlds are not for everyone – and they're not going to be the first social media tool you go for. While in some ways a virtual world is just another social network – albeit one with a rich 3D graphical interface – the barriers to using them are considerable. You first have to download the software and learn the interface.

Why virtual worlds work for business

Second Life works for business in the same way any social network does. People make connections with each other in Second Life and build up lists of friends and join groups related to their interests. As with any social network, if your community of interest is in SL, then you should be too.

Second Life can be used for business in the following ways:

1 **Developing products.** Second Life can be useful for creating 3-D representations of your products, which can be useful for prototyping products inexpensively and getting valuable market research feedback, whether they're eco-homes, a new mass transit system – or wind-up toys, as successfully trialled in SL by Little Wonders Studio (http://littlewonderstudio.com).

2 **Promoting real-life products.** Fashion designers have sold virtual clothing as a way of promoting real-life brands; but you could also set up (virtual) shop with click-throughs from virtual products to real products on your website. How about selling virtual jewellery for avatars – but also offering real-life jewellery via links from your virtual shop to your e-commerce website? Ideally your brand should work in both SL and in the real world.

3 **Promoting real-life services.** You can promote your services in a variety of ways, including putting up virtual posters and organising events or seminars. This can work well if you have a techy service to offer.

4 **Selling virtual products**. It is also possible to make a living in SL by selling purely virtual products. Anything you create in SL, using its own scripting language, you own the intellectual property to, and can sell in-world. Residents in SL customise their avatars by buying not only clothing but also skin, hair, body shapes and gestures such as dance moves. The in-world currency is Linden Dollars (L$) – but these can be exchanged on the 'Lindex' – a market-driven currency exchange – for real cash. At the time of writing the exchange rate is around L$250 to the US$.

5 **Selling virtual land**. This is how Anshe Chung made her millions. And that's millions of US dollars, not Linden dollars. Anshe Chung is the avatar of Ailin Graef – a former school and college teacher. She has built an online business around the development and brokerage of virtual land in Second Life – a business that has made her a US millionaire, and got her on to the front cover of *Business Week* in 2006. In 2004 she began selling and creating custom animations and then used this money to buy and develop virtual land. She now owns hundreds of servers' worth of land, most of which are sold or rented to other users as a part of her 'Dreamland' areas. In November 2006 Chung announced that she had become the first online personality to achieve a net worth exceeding one million US dollars from profits entirely earned inside a virtual world. Anshe Chung's business now employs more than 80 people full time, most of them programmers and artists. She counts several Fortune 100 companies among her clients. And all this was achieved over a period of two and a half years, and from an initial investment of $10. Virtual world, virtual land: real money.

6 **Meeting clients and suppliers**. If you have clients or suppliers in SL – or if you want to find some – it is possible to do business in SL by having meetings. This can be useful if you want to get together a group of people from around the world. Yes, you could do this using Skype or videoconferencing, but the experience of meeting someone in SL as your avatar is qualitatively different.

7 **Training**. The experience of virtual interaction with people is one reason why education works well in SL – not just for university courses, but also for seminars, workshops, and sales meetings. If your business involves any form of training, and you have a market in SL, consider running a seminar there. You can even stream in PowerPoint slides, audio and video.

Thousands of residents make part or all of their real-life income from their Second Life businesses. Some of these include:

- party and wedding planner
- fashion designer
- custom avatar designer
- jewellery maker
- architect
- fine artist
- musician
- publisher
- writer
- publicist.

See more at: http://secondlife.com/whatis/businesses.php.

---

virtual worlds in action

Virtual Farmers Market (www.vfmuk.com)

Marcus Carter has taken a novel approach to virtual world marketing. Instead of trying to tap into an existing community on Second Life, he has created his own community around his business, facilitated by his very own, bespoke virtual world: the Virtual Farmers Market.

figure 14.1 Virtual Farmers Market

> Built using the Unity gaming platform (http://unity3d.com), this is on a smaller scale than Second Life, but is a similar 3D graphical representation of a farmers' market, where customers can walk around – and they can interact with the suppliers, who are based in the UK and Ireland, by clicking on a stall to be taken to the relevant part of the website, where food producers explain more about their wares via video.
>
> Speaking on BBC Radio 4's *Food Programme* in March 2010, three months after launch, he described it as 'an alternative for people who haven't got time to go to a real-life farmers' market, and therefore miss out on some great food. It's hard for a small food company to make a big noise online. If you make a really nice chilli jam and launch a website, it's very hard to get people to come to your website as one producer with one product. So I'm trying to form a collection of 55 of the UK's best producers, so that people can come and find them, learn about the food, and then go on and shop with everything into one basket and have it delivered to your home.' Many of the independent food producers don't even have their own website, so this is a way for them to come together to reach a national audience online.
>
> Through the virtual interface and video material, Virtual Farmers Market replicates the experience of visiting a farmers' market as closely as is possible online. It works for the same reason many other forms of online marketing work for a small business: by building trust, and communicating authentically and directly with customers. This is what has helped drive orders – even from customers who were previously distrustful of online shopping. The videos really get across the personalities of the food producers, and help build a connection with the product: 'You're not buying Dave's chilli oil, you're buying Dave and his chilli oil.'
>
> **Get the idea**: Creating your own virtual world is more complex than using Second Life, but can be an effective way to provide a rich shopping interface for your customers that is closely tied to your website. When thinking virtually, don't limit yourself to the video game style interface provided: use video material and click-throughs to further information on your website to enhance the experience.

Get up to speed with virtual worlds

We will focus on Second Life for the rest of this chapter. These are the steps you need to follow.

1 Download Second Life and create an account.

2 Customise your avatar.

3 Build a community of contacts.

4 Buying land, virtual architecture and scripting.

Download Second Life and create an account

Sign up for a free account at http://secondlife.com, and download the soft-ware. You can upgrade later to a paid-for premium account that allows you to own land and build on if you want – but you're unlikely to need this to start with. Every avatar has a unique name that is different to your real name. When you sign up, you can choose from a long but restricted list of last names, and any first name you wish, so long as your full avatar name is available. My avatar name is Jon Kerang. You need to know that if you want to find me in SL – it's a bit like a username.

ff every avatar has a unique name that is different to your real name ff

When you start out in SL, you're first sent to Welcome Island to learn the basics of SL – how to walk, talk, stand/sit, use the camera controls, fly and teleport. Everything you need to get around and use the platform.

figure 14.2 Second Life Welcome Island

For many years, people communicated in SL via text-based chat – like instant messaging. Then in 2007, voice was introduced. Residents can wear a headset in real life, and speak normally in Second Life – a bit like using Skype. But the immersive 3D sound design means that if someone approaches you from the side, they sound in the right place.

Once you have learned the basics, you're released into Second Life. You can search for places to visit using the search button at the bottom of your screen – and then teleport there. You can also search for groups and people. Second Life is built on islands. That's not a metaphor – they are literally virtual representations of tropical islands, complete with beaches, palm trees and seagulls. Plus anything that people have built on them.

To find out more about what SL looks like before signing up for an account, do a search for 'Second Life' on YouTube – there are plenty of 'machinima' to be found there – videos made within SL. The London School of Journalism, for example, videos their lectures within SL and puts them on YouTube.

Customise your avatar

One of the first things you are likely to want to do in Second Life is to go shopping! You start your Second Life with a basic avatar, but you may want to change the looks Linden gave you. Click on the Search button at the bottom of your screen to search for 'clothing', or whatever you want to buy for your avatar to find a likely list of shops and islands. Don't forget you can also buy body shapes, skins and hair. Although you can edit your appearance manually, you are much better off buying a professionally designed look. And if you want to look just how you do in real life, there are people in SL who will design you a photorealistic avatar, if you supply good-quality images.

There are various 'freebie' islands in SL where you can acquire free clothing and other items. Anything you buy – or are given – appears in your Inventory.

Update your profile details by selecting 'Profile...' from the Edit menu. This is the SL equivalent of filling in your personal profile, and you have the opportunity to include groups you are a member of, your interests, a profile image and a paragraph of blurb about you – for both your Second Life and your First Life – and a web address. Be sure to include your business website here.

Build a community of contacts

Search for groups in your area of interest, check out the islands on which they are based, subscribe to the group's newsletter, attend any events that are running there, and start making contacts. If you already know other people who are in SL, do a search for their avatar name and click 'Add Friend...'

Buying land, virtual architecture and scripting

The more advanced topics of buying land, creating buildings and other objects in SL are beyond the scope of this book. But, as you make connections in SL, you are likely to come across people who can help you. You can even place an ad in SL's classified listings via the screen where you edit your profile.

quick win

Using posters and dispensers

If there is a community in Second Life that seems relevant to your business, there is a very easy way to promote yourself to its members without terraforming an island, or hiring a virtual architect. First of all, find your community by doing a keyword search in SL, and look for those groups related to your business that have the largest population size. Very often they will be based on a specific island within SL, and there are likely to be advertising opportunities on the islands.

The cheapest and easiest options are posters or dispensers. A poster is literally a virtual poster or billboard that you can put on the wall of the building in SL for a specified time (where the person who manages the island permits it). Sometimes you will see 'advertise here' messages on buildings, sometimes you will need to approach the person who runs the island direct. Have a graphic designer produce a poster for you promoting your business to the size and format specified. Submit it to the island owner along with a link to your website. When someone touches your poster in SL, they will then click through to your website. You can measure the effectiveness of this by using a tracking link or unique landing page.

figure 14.3 A dispenser on Cookie Island

The other option is to use a dispenser. This is the only form of advertising I use in SL. A dispenser is a graphical representation of the newspaper dispenser, and works well for promoting blogs. There is a large and active community of writers in SL in a group called The Written Word, based on Cookie Island. I have a *Publishing Talk* dispenser in the main square of Cookie Island which says 'Touch here for the latest edition'. When someone touches the dispenser they click through to the *Publishing Talk* blog. There are additional dispensers in virtual bookshops on the island and elsewhere in SL.

Manage the workload

You don't need to spend a lot of time in SL. Even if you own an office building or shop that gets a lot of passing trade, you can automate it and don't need to staff it by being there, unless you have a specific event or launch party to host. Shops run themselves in SL – people click on items to buy them.

It is not worth your time learning how to script objects in SL, unless you are truly fascinated by it. Hire a programmer or virtual architect who can create objects and buildings to your design.

Measure your results

Your metrics in SL may include the number of:

- Residents in a group you create.
- Click-throughs to your website from a poster or other in-world object.
- Residents who attend your party, seminar or other event.
- Views of a YouTube video created as a 'machinima' within SL.

Take action

▪ **Sign** up to Second Life.

▪ **Customise** your avatar.

▪ **Join** some groups and make connections.

▪ **Investigate** advertising opportunities in-world, such as posters, dispensers, classified ads and ads in in-world newspapers.

▪ **Consider** whether it is worth owning land and setting up shop in SL.

Pass it on

How to be discovered on social bookmarking sites

O nce you've created your website, search engine marketing (SEM) will help people find it on Google and other search engines (see Chapter 4). But there's another way people can discover your content and therefore your business: using social bookmarking sites. The reason for creating the content you produced in Part 3 – blogs, podcasts, video and images – was to create something of value for your community that will draw them on to your site *and that they will want to pass on and share*. Although you can – and should – promote that content yourself, nothing beats your community passing it on for you. This chapter will show you how to make it easy for them to do so.

What is social bookmarking?

Have you come across a website you liked recently, and saved it to the 'bookmarks' on your browser so you could easily find it again later? It's a handy feature that all browsers come with. Social bookmarking is exactly the same – except that you do it in public. Because you can also add notes and keyword tags to the pages you save, other people can use social bookmarking sites to find links that other people have saved. Social bookmarking is therefore a form of social search – an approach to searching where the best web pages are chosen by humans rather than computer algorithms.

> **ff** social bookmarking is a form of social search **JJ**

Three of the most popular social bookmarking sites are Delicious, Digg and StumbleUpon. Each takes a slightly different approach to bookmarking.

Why social bookmarking works for business

There are two ways you can use social bookmarking sites to enhance the discoverability of your content – and therefore your business:

1 Bookmark web pages you think will be interesting to your community.

2 Encourage others to bookmark your web pages with social bookmarking buttons.

If you bookmark web pages yourself, you can build up a useful resource of sites and pages that is useful to your community, and will draw them on to your own site. You can create a basic profile on all these sites, and connect with others. If you include your business website on your profile, it's another way to lead people back on to your site.

And once you've created such a resource, you can pull your latest saved links back on to your website in the form of a widget, leveraging your workload, keeping your content fresh, giving people another reason to visit your site.

You can also use these sites as 'listening tools' to find out which pieces of your content people are saving, and what they are saying about you. You can find out which content items are most popular, which will give you feedback on which types of content you should create.

But the biggest business benefit to social bookmarking sites is that they facilitate the 'pass-on-ability' of your content. While not everyone will share your content with others, those that do are likely to be active in the social media space, and be a trusted voice within their own online community. They are 'sneezers' – active content consumers who will translate and repeat your message to their friends. That's a very powerful form of word of mouth marketing. Tap into it by participating in social bookmarking sites, and making it easy for your fans to spread the word by using social bookmarking buttons that encourage people not only to save your web pages to Delicious, Digg, StumbleUpon, etc., but also to take actions such as 'Tweet this', 'Share on Facebook' and more.

> **❝ sneezers – active content consumers who will translate and repeat your message ❞**

BBQ Addicts (www.bbqaddicts.com)

Jason Day and Aaron Chronister have turned their passion for barbeques into a business. They run a website called BBQ Addicts from Kansas City, featuring recipes, reviews and products relating to barbequing. They had a massive spike in traffic to their website, thanks to a recipe widely shared on social bookmarking sites.

It started with a tweet from a bacon lover asking what the barbequers could do with bacon. The 'Bacon Explosion' was born – a 5,000 calorie bacon-stuffed, bacon-wrapped Italian sausage with Kansas City barbeque sauce, smoked in a blend of oak and hickory wood. The recipe appeared on their website two days before Christmas 2008 (www.bbqaddicts.com/blog/recipes/bacon-explosion). On Christmas Day, traffic spiked to 27,000 visitors[7]. Within a month, the site had 16,000 sites linking to it and hundreds of thousands of visitors[8] – traffic that is vital for their advertising revenue as well as the products they sell.

How was this achieved, and in such a short timescale? They tweeted about the recipe to their 1,200 followers, and used other social networks to share the recipe. But Aaron says that the main driver of traffic was social bookmarking sites – particularly StumbleUpon, a site that serves up content to match people's interests. Each post on the site includes links to 'Stumble it', 'Digg this', 'Tweet this' and 'Add to Delicious' to encourage people to spread the word. The recipe appeared on the front page of StumbleUpon for three days.

The phenomenon was then picked up by traditional media, and reported in the *New York Times*, on CNN, Fox News, *Good Morning America* and more, creating more exposure for them and their site. The recipe has become so popular that they now also sell a range of heat-and-eat versions of the Bacon Explosion from their website – and their new-found fame has led to a recipe book, *BBQ Makes Everything Better* (Scribner, May 2010).

Of course, the real secret of their success was to have some compelling content that people wanted to share in the first place – and there's really no substitute for that. The 'extreme' nature of the recipe, and its timing around the holiday season, helped too. But by making that content easy to share on social networks and social bookmarking sites, it was possible to capitalise on that interest, generate a vast amount of web traffic – and then build on that success.

Get the idea: Make sure you use social bookmarking buttons on all your blog posts to make it easy for your visitors to share your content. But always remember that you must also create compelling content that people will want to share.

7 http://www.nytimes.com/2009/01/28/dining/28bacon.html?_r=2&em
8 http://swissmoneyblog.com/2009/01/29/a-delicious-internet-marketing-case-study-unless-youre-a-vegetarian/

Get up to speed with social bookmarking

Experiment with a few different social bookmarking sites to see how they might work for you. But the most important thing to do is to enable people to easily share your content, such as your blog posts, on social bookmarking sites *and* on their networks such as Facebook, Twitter, LinkedIn.

1 Save some sites to Delicious.

2 Digg for victory.

3 StumbleUpon some new sites.

4 Add social bookmarking buttons to your blog.

Save some sites to Delicious

Sign up for an account with www.delicious.com. Be sure to include your business website in your profile, as this will show up on the list of bookmarks you have saved.

figure 15.1 Publishing Talk's Delicious bookmarks

Install the toolbar on your browser. When you want to add a site to Delicious, you can either do this on the Delicious site itself, or simply go to the site you want to save, and click the TAG button on your toolbar.

figure 15.2 The Delicious toolbar

The following dialogue box pops up. Add a title, some notes if you want, and be sure to add some tags, as this will help people find the site you've bookmarked. Delicious will suggest some for you, but you can add your own.

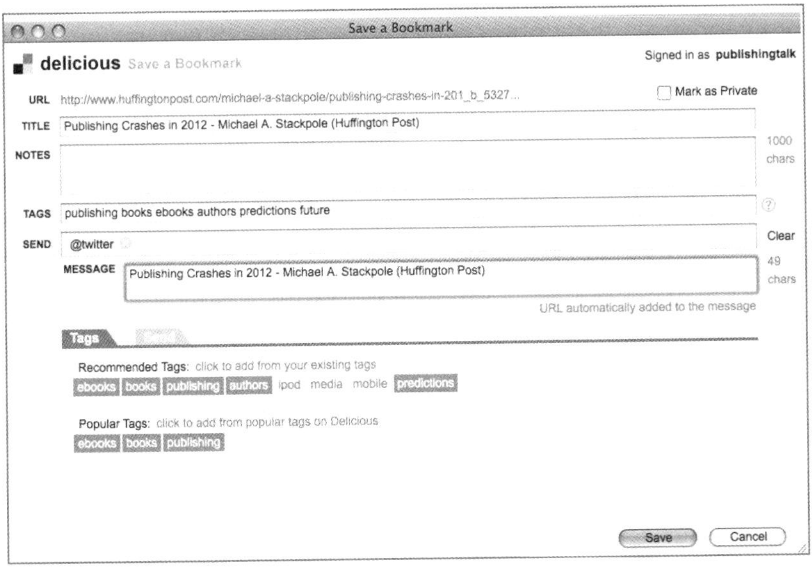

figure 15.3 Saving a bookmark to Delicious

Link your Delicious account to Twitter, and when you click Save, you also automatically tweet the link. Delicious adds its own shortened 'icio.us' URL.

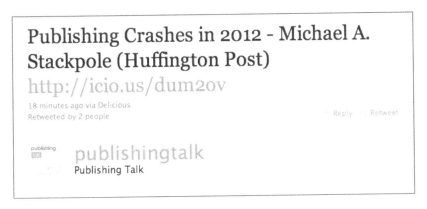

figure 15.4 A tweeted Delicious link

This can therefore be a way for people to share as well as bookmark content. As with all social bookmarking tools you can bookmark your own content as well as other people's – but don't do this excessively, and make sure you bookmark plenty of other people's sites too. Your goal is really to become part of the community, and make it easy for that community to bookmark your content.

quick win

Add your Delicious links to your blog or website

The sites you save can be a useful resource for your community, which draws them from Delicious onto your blog or website. And with the tools Delicious provides, you can also create an instant list of interesting sites for your community right on your blog. This keeps your content fresh and gives people another reason to keep coming back to your blog.

- Go to http://delicious.com/help/tools to find the tools you can use to promote your Delicious feed.

- Select Linkrolls (http://delicious.com/help/linkrolls) for a bit of HTML code that you can add to your blog or website to display the latest pages you have bookmarked in Delicious.

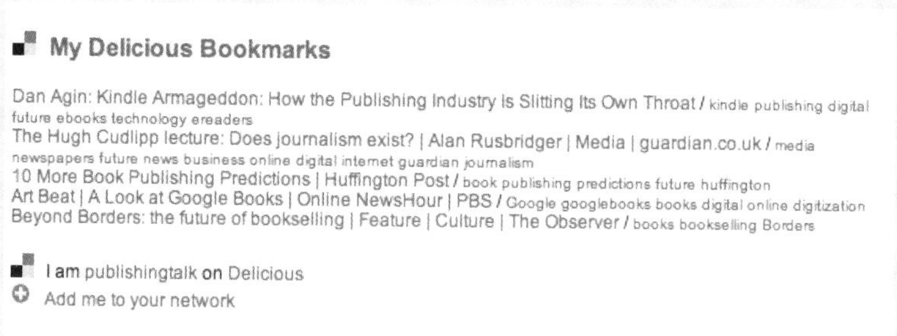

■ **My Delicious Bookmarks**

Dan Agin: Kindle Armageddon: How the Publishing Industry Is Slitting Its Own Throat / kindle publishing digital future ebooks technology ereaders
The Hugh Cudlipp lecture: Does journalism exist? | Alan Rusbridger | Media | guardian.co.uk / media newspapers future news business online digital internet guardian journalism
10 More Book Publishing Predictions | Huffington Post / book publishing predictions future huffington
Art Beat | A Look at Google Books | Online NewsHour | PBS / Google googlebooks books digital online digitization
Beyond Borders: the future of bookselling | Feature | Culture | The Observer / books bookselling Borders

■ I am publishingtalk on Delicious
✪ Add me to your network

---

figure 15.5 A Delicious Linkroll

- Alternatively, select Tagrolls (http://delicious.com/help/tagrolls) to display a tag cloud of keywords with which you have tagged the sites you have saved. Tags are displayed in larger text the more frequently they are used. Clicking on any of these words will link to a list of web pages you have saved and tagged with that keyword.

■ My Delicious Tags

ABI author authors blogging book bookdeal **books** bookselling bookswap Borders **business** businessmodel careers CBS copyright **digital** digitization e-books e-readers **ebooks** eco economics engine **ereaders** event facebook **future** **google** googlebooks green guardian hachette house huffington industry **internet** iPod jobs journalism keitai **kindle** Letterman literary **literature** **marketing** mashable McCain **media** mobile murdoch newfacebook **news** newscorp newspapers nymag online paper predictions **pricing** profile publishers **publishing** random Reader reading recession recruitment research revenue **search** sector self-publishing sethgodin sexism **shosetsu** skills socialmedia socialnetworking **sony** strategy survey sustainable **technology** time **trends** Twitter video web writing YouTube zuckerberg

■ I am publishingtalk on Delicious
○ Add me to your network

figure 15.6 A Delicious Tagroll

Digg for victory

Digg is like an online newspaper, and is sometimes called a 'social news site'. Instead of an editor choosing the front page, and what goes in the various sections – such as Business & Finance, Technology or Arts & Culture – it is the readers who decide what content is included – from news to articles to video and images. This content is not created by Digg, but submitted from all over the Internet by Digg users, by clicking on a 'Digg this' button next to a piece of web content such as a blog post. The more votes or 'Diggs' an item gets, the more visible it becomes on Digg. Story popularity can go down as well as up, as users can also vote to 'Bury' an item if they don't like it. The ones with the most votes appear on the front page – though this is very hard to achieve. If you do make it to the front page, expect to attract a significant amount of web traffic back to your site – potentially tens of thousands of visitors in a single day.

❝ Digg is like an online newspaper, and is sometimes called a 'social news site' ❞

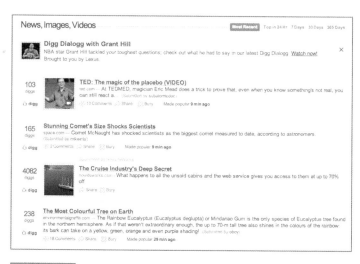

Digg is also a social network, in the sense that you can add a profile and connect with friends. Be sure to fill in your profile and include a link to your business website. To get the most out of Digg, participate in the community by Digging other people's content (not just your own!), and connecting with other users that share your interests. You can also connect with your Facebook account to automatically add those Facebook friends who already use Digg to your friends list, and to post your Digg activity in your Facebook feed.

> **❝ certain categories are more popular on Digg, particularly anything techy ❞**

You can, and should, submit your own content to Digg. Make sure the content you submit will be of interest to a large number of people on Digg, and fits into their subject categories. Choose your best content items – not every single blog post. Certain categories are more popular on Digg, particularly anything techy.

The first step is to log in to Digg, click the **Submit New** link at the top of the page, and then enter the URL of the content you're submitting. Specify whether this is a News Article, Video or Image.

figure 15.8 Submit news, video or images to Digg

You then need to add a title and description and choose a category. Space is limited here, so make sure you write a good title that will encourage people to click on it. Often people will Digg content based on the title alone. Like blog articles, titles that grab attention include 'how to' and list-based articles, such as '10 ways to...'

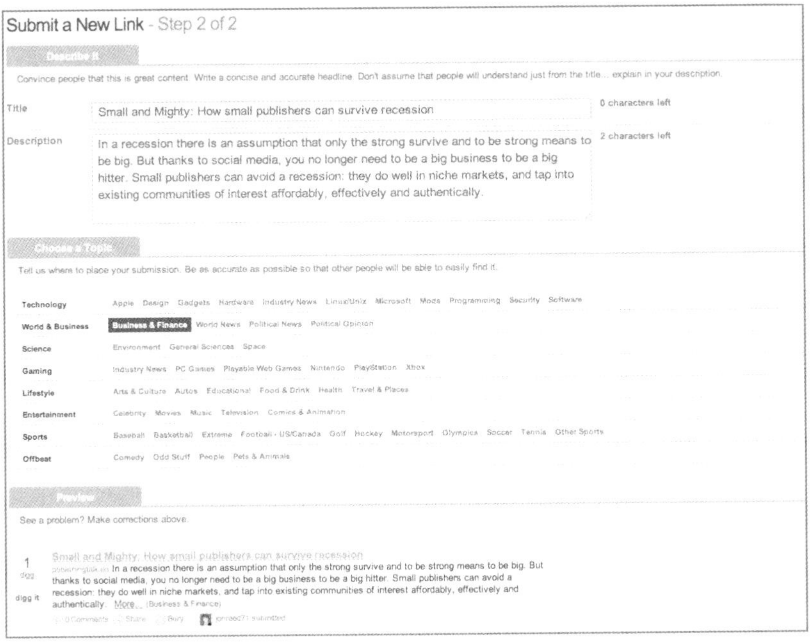

figure 15.9 Submit a link to Digg

Once you've started Digging some articles, as with Delicious, you can pull in the latest stories you've Dugg on to your blog with a widget. In fact, you can choose what to show from a wide variety of variables. I would suggest doing it by your username.

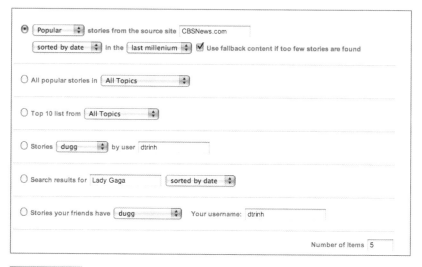

figure 15.10 Create a Digg widget

figure 15.11 A Digg widget

StumbleUpon some new sites

If Digg is a social news site, StumbleUpon is a social discovery site, with around 9 million members who are basically channel surfing through the Internet. When you sign up to an account with StumbleUpon, you are invited to choose from a wide range of topics that interest you. You can update this any time at http://www.stumbleupon.com/settings/interests, and StumbleUpon also learns what you like. One of the interest category lists is 'Suggested'.

Install the browser toolbar, and you have a range of new buttons to help you Stumble. The **Stumble!** button simply opens a random web page that may interest you. This is based on your interests, and the popularity of the page with other Stumblers.

The default setting is 'All' – i.e. all the interests you have entered – but you can narrow the search down by selecting a single topic, such as Entrepreneurship. The thumbs-up and thumbs-down buttons allow you to vote on pages, and helps StumbleUpon learn your preferences.

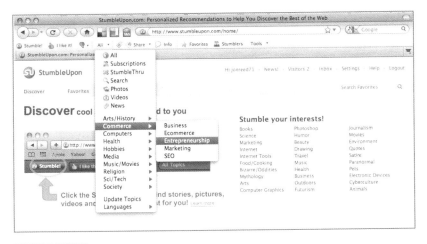

figure 15.12 StumbleUpon

Whenever you thumbs-up a web page, it appears in your favourites at www.stumbleupon.com/favorites. You can also add descriptions ('reviews') and tags to the pages you save.

Like Digg, you can make friends on StumbleUpon – though they're called 'subscribers'. A list of your subscribers and subscriptions (people whose favourites you have subscribed to) appears in your profile. To find people to subscribe to, start by thumbs-upping content you like, and click the **Info** button on your StumbleUpon toolbar to see who else liked that page – and consider subscribing to them. They are likely to be interested in the same things you are, and content that you submit. And if they visit your profile and click the **Stumble** button, they will be shown only sites that you have thumbed-up – which may include your own content. You can submit content via the StumbleUpon site as well as by thumbs-upping it from your toolbar.

StumbleUpon has one big advantage over Digg: it is easier to generate web traffic. Whereas Digg is rather feast or famine – you get vast amounts of traffic for a few days if you make it to the front page, and very little if you don't – StumbleUpon builds your traffic over time as more people give you the thumbs up. And if you want more traffic from StumbleUpon, you can pay for it with ads at https://www.stumbleupon.com/ads, targeted at visitors' areas of interest.

> ❝ StumbleUpon has one big advantage over Digg: it is easier to generate web traffic ❞

Add social bookmarking buttons to your blog

Participating in social bookmarking communities is one way of encouraging people to pass on your content. But the most effective thing you can do to encourage your content to be shared on social bookmarking sites – apart from creating compelling, remarkable content – is to add some buttons to the bottom of every blog post. These enable people to submit your content to the social sites they use without having to go to the site and enter the details manually.

There are many WordPress plugins that will do this for you, and provide dozens of alternative buttons to choose from. I like one called Sexy Bookmarks (http://wordpress.org/extend/plugins/sexybookmarks), which has nicely styled buttons with drop-shadows that pop up when you hover over them. You can display as many as you like, but I use a single row of buttons to keep things uncluttered and focus on the sites I'm most interested in being promoted on: Twitter, Facebook, LinkedIn, MySpace, FriendFeed, Delicious, Digg, StumbleUpon and Technorati.

figure 15.13 Sexy Bookmarks – a WordPress plugin to display social bookmarks on your blog posts

The newest button to appear on these plugins is the Google Buzz button – which is used to share content with Gmail and Google Reader users. Some plugins display text instead of graphical buttons; some, including Sexy Bookmarks, show text such as 'Tweet this', 'Share on Facebook', 'Digg this', etc. when you hover over the buttons. You can also add the Digg button to your site which people can click on to increase your Digg votes without even leaving your site.

Using TweetMeme (www.tweetmeme.com), you can also display a 'retweet' button at the top of your blog post, and have access to additional metrics on the TweetMeme site.

figure 15.14 TweetMeme retweet button

This is a bit like Digg for Twitter, since it displays how many people have retweeted the content using the service, and TweetMeme also has a front page and categories displaying the most popular articles retweeted. ShareThis (http://sharethis.com) is also popular, and also keeps a tally of the number of 'shares' or a particular piece of content.

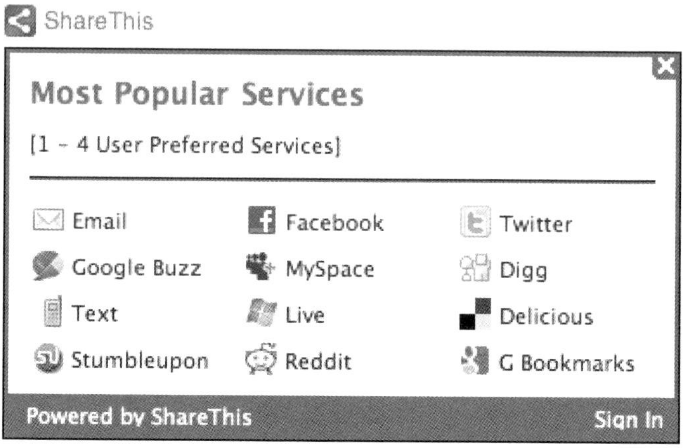

figure 15.15 ShareThis

Whichever option you choose, make sure you make it easy for your community to pass on and share your content.

figure 15.16 Recent links on TweetMeme

Manage the workload

Don't feel you have to use every social bookmarking site – or indeed any at all. The most important thing is to enable others to bookmark your content easily using social bookmarking buttons. That's as easy as installing a WordPress plugin, and only needs doing once.

If you do want to bookmark sites yourself, choose one that you like and stick to it. It is better to build up a comprehensive list of useful links than spread yourself too thinly across all the sites. And once you've started to create a useful resource, repurpose it by pulling in the Delicious bookmarks you've saved or the stories you've Dugg into your blog with a widget.

Measure your results

Most of the social bookmarking sites have some way of measuring how often your content appeared on them. Simply doing a search for your business, brand, blog or website will show you how many people have bookmarked your content.

Delicious gives you plenty of drill-down detail, and can be useful as a listening tool: to find out what other people are saying about you. Do a search on the Delicious site for your business and see which of your content items are the most popular, who bookmarked them, what tags they used, and how they described them. This can give you some ideas about which of your blog posts are the most popular – so you can write more like that.

❝ Delicious can be useful as a listening tool ❞

StumbleUpon has analytics available at http://su.pr. This helps you track the performance of your posts in real time, view your traffic, clicks, referrers, Stumbles, and retweets in one place.

If you're interested in who is tweeting your content, the most sophisticated analytics are offered by TweetMeme Analytics (http://tweetmeme.com/about/analytics). This enables you to discover how your content has spread through Twitter, which path it took, who retweeted it, which Twitter users were most influential in retweeting your content, which retweets resulted in more click-throughs to your content and more. This detailed information will give you valuable feedback for improving the performance of your content on Twitter.

Your main aim is to get people to share your stuff. These metrics will all help you measure how successful you have been at persuading them to do so.

Take action

◼ **Save** some sites to Delicious, Digg and StumbleUpon.

◼ **Choose** which social bookmarking site(s) you will use, and create a widget for your blog.

◼ **Add** social bookmarking buttons to your blog.

◼ **Consider** using the TweetMeme button and TweetMeme Analytics to see how your content spreads on Twitter.

◼ **Create** compelling content that people will want to pass on.

Get help

16

Do you need a consultant?

How to find someone to help you achieve your vision

There is a huge amount you can do yourself to promote your business online, cheaply, easily and effectively. It is good to do many things yourself, such as writing blog posts and status updates, to retain your own authentic, personal voice. But it doesn't hurt to call in a bit of help when you need it – either to help you plan your marketing, do the technical media production tasks, or simply to save time that you could better spend doing what you do best – running your business. Follow the advice of management guru Peter Drucker: 'Do what you do best, and outsource the rest.'

> ❝ it doesn't hurt to call in a bit of help when you need it ❞

But first, a word of caution. There are an awful lot of marketing consultants out there. How do you cut through the hyperbole and inflated claims and decide who is worth your time and hard-earned money? In particular, in the past couple of years, a plethora of social media consultants have appeared. It's getting so that the term 'social media consultant' is attracting negative connotations, even though it is the most accurate description of what some of us do. Some consultants do great work for their clients. Some are more hype than help. Some people will tell you they can make you fabulously wealthy with little or no effort. This is unlikely. Some will promise to boost your Twitter followers by extraordinary volumes, often using illegal automated scripts or 'bots'.

Some will offer to manage your social media presence or ghost-write your blog. While this may work for some people, I would be very cautious about handing over my online reputation to someone else. I have a very particular voice and style online – and it is likely that you do too, unless your online personality is very bland and corporate.

Some search engine marketing consultants will tell you they can make you appear as the top search result on Google. And they may be able to – briefly – before you are booted off Google for trying to game the system. If something sounds too good to be true, guess what? It probably is.

Here are some questions you should ask before hiring a consultant:

- What projects have you worked on previously for which clients?
- What benefits did you bring to them?
- What metrics would you use to measure results?
- Do you have your own blog/podcast/Twitter feed, etc.? How successful is it?
- What specific tasks can you help with?

Online marketing is powerful – but it is not witchcraft. There are no Da Vinci Code style 'secrets' of online marketing that you need to pay a fortune to discover, having read someone's lengthy online sales letter or 'squeeze page'.

While you might want to kick-start your marketing by having someone draw up a marketing plan for you, in many cases it is not necessary to hire a consultant. It is better to brush up on the principles and practices, and familiarise yourself with those online marketing tools that seem most suited to your business. After all, you are the one who will be tweeting/blogging/AudioBooing, etc. And if you follow the advice in the 'Manage the workload' sections of this book, you are less likely to be overwhelmed by the responsibility. Reading this book is, of course, a great start, and there are more resources, such as video tutorials, on the website at www.getuptospeed.biz.

But even if, having read this book, you decide you want to hire others to do the work for you, the knowledge you have gained of the principles and processes will help you commission the work more effectively. There are a number of scenarios when you might want to hire someone to help with your online marketing:

1 You're an experienced web designer/blogger/podcaster/video producer, etc. – but you're spending too much time on media production when you should be focusing on your businesss.

2 Your blog/podcast etc. has come to a standstill because you no longer have the time or interest to do it all yourself.

3 You or your team are overwhelmed by the additional workload and responsibility of maintaining your online marketing.

4 You're new to all this, and don't know where to begin.

The sort of help you hire will depend on the size of your organisation, and the sort of tasks you need doing.

Audit your tasks

The first stage is to identify what needs doing and where the gaps are. Draw up a task list, and decide which things can be done in-house and which you want to outsource. Which tasks do you, realistically, have the time to do alongside your other responsibilities? Which tasks are critical to be done in-house to maintain your unique personal voice and brand? Where does your expertise lie, and which tasks would be better outsourced to a specialist?

> **❝ the first stage is to identify what needs doing and where the gaps are ❞**

You can do this at the level of your entire marketing plan, or for a specific project such as producing a podcast. Tasks can then be broken down into smaller chunks than 'produce a podcast'. You might, for example, want to record interviews, but then hand over the raw files to an audio producer who can edit them, add some music and output them as discrete MP3 files – and then take it back in-house to upload to your blog yourself.

Think about the roles that relate to each task (whether in-house or outsourced), and who will own each one. Draw up a grid a little like this:

Role	Task	Owner
Strategy	Draw up an online marketing plan for new product launch	
Graphic design	Design a podcover Create a web design concept for a new blog Design email newsletter template	
Editorial	Write blog posts Subedit blog posts from contributors Conduct interviews for podcast	
Web design/ Development	Create bespoke WordPress theme for blog Create ecommerce site Create bespoke Facebook app	
Production	Audio editing and post-production of podcasts Edit video clips	
Admin	Set up accounts on Twitter, Facebook, LinkedIn Set up Twitterfeed for blog Sort out email newsletter databases	
Monitoring	Collate web-stat reports and metrics from Facebook, YouTube, TweetMeme Analytics	

When to hire a social media manager

Many organisations have been experimenting with social media for a while in a fairly uncoordinated way – which is fine to start with, as most of this stuff is free, and that can be a good way to find out what works for you. But at some point, it can become hard to maintain all the blogs and updates, effort may be duplicated, and a proliferation of accounts confusing if people are just going off and doing their own thing. At some stage, some order needs restoring.

If you work for a large organisation and have reached a critical mass of social media being created and maintained that becomes hard to keep track of, it may be time to consider hiring a social media manager. This is someone who can work across an organisation, coordinate roles and responsibilities, help draw up strategies and marketing plans, and assist with the actual work of maintaining blogs, podcasts, video and social media sites. He or she may also hire in technical or production help where needed.

Alternatively, you may opt for a committee-based solution: appoint a committee of existing staff whose role it is to draw up a corporate level social media marketing plan, with clear aims and objectives; and then draw up some guidelines and policies. These should state how various tools – such as Twitter – are used by the organisation, and who is responsible for what. Include also any naming conventions to be used if there are many Twitter or Facebook accounts to be used across the organisation.

When to hire a virtual assistant

If you are a start-up or entrepreneur, you probably won't have the luxury of a social media manager. It will probably all be down to you. That's not a bad thing, as social media often works best for small businesses. However, before you despair of the enormous workload and learning curve before you, don't worry: I'm not suggesting you do it all yourself. You can hire in help quite cheaply – and a virtual assistant (VA) can be a great asset to a small business. And not just for marketing, but also all sorts of tasks.

> **a virtual assistant can be a great asset to a small business**

In his bestselling book *The 4-Hour Workweek*, Tim Ferriss advocates outsourcing as a means of leveraging your time and resources via 'geo-arbitrage'. That means 'exploiting global pricing and currency differences for profit or lifestyle purposes' – or charging your clients in pounds or dollars and paying your suppliers pesos or rupees. Examples he cites of outsourcing companies you can use to achieve this include Brickwork India (www.brickworkindia.com), based in Bangalore, India's 'Silicone Valley', which specialises in Remote Executive Assistants who can perform a wide variety of tasks on a time zone to suit you.

The outsourcing revolution has moved on a little since then: we've had a banking collapse, and global pricing has shifted slightly. India and the Philippines are still great value, and there are talented technical experts to be found who speak excellent English. But it is also easier than ever to find VAs all over the world for a reasonable price, including in the USA, which some people prefer for geographical reasons.

A VA can take on a wide range of tasks remotely, from maintaining blogs to doing market research to audio editing to helping with email newsletters. There are plenty of tasks and functions where it makes more sense to get someone else to do, in order to save you time and have them done with more expertise than you possess.

It can be alarming at first handing over control to someone at a remote location – especially when you hand over logins and passwords – but you will soon reap the benefits of not doing it all yourself. It pays to draw up very detailed instructions, even process flowcharts, for specific tasks that need doing. Many people also use Camtasia (the screen capture software mentioned in Chapter 8) to record online tasks such as blog maintenance. It can be a very quick way of communicating, on screen, exactly what you need doing.

When to hire a technical expert

You can also hire in technical experts for specialist functions such as video production, graphic design and web design. Your VA can probably help you outsource these tasks too, if they are beyond his/her skillset.

For example, I don't claim to be a graphic designer – I always outsource these tasks to freelancers who are far more talented than me. I can design websites, but I rarely do these days – I outsource web design to save my time for things that it is better spent on – such as developing my business, running workshops and writing.

Where to find help

The best advice I can give you is to use Elance (www.elance.com) rather than searching for outsourcing companies based in specific countries. This is a global online marketplace that matches up freelancers and outsourcers for just about any job you can think of. Simply post the job you want doing, and sit back and wait for the bids to come in from all over the world. Some bids will be from individuals, and some will be specialist outsourcing or VA companies with whom you may subsequently develop an ongoing business relationship. Pick the one you want to work with, and pay their fee in advance via your PayPal account. It is held 'in escrow' until the job is completed to your satisfaction. A rating and reviews system maintains the quality of suppliers, and provides useful reviews of jobs completed.

The vast array of tasks you can outsource this way includes:

Web design

Blog development, maintenance and writing

SEM/SEO

Banner ads

Graphic design

Email newsletter maintenance and writing

Audio editing and transcription

Market research

Business plans

Marketing plans

Recruitment

Virtual assistant/administrative tasks

...and many more. See a list of the top 100 jobs you can Elance at www.elance.com/p/100-projects-outsource.html.

Manage your outsourced projects

Sometimes outsourcing is a simple matter of finding the right person with the technical expertise you need for your project, and then working closely with them until it is delivered. Sometimes it is an ongoing relationship, such as with a VA. Sometimes, for large projects involving several people, some more sophisticated project management is required.

I'm based in London yet have outsourced tasks to people based overseas, including in the USA. I also regularly use freelancers based in the UK, many of whom I almost never meet in person. I keep in touch by email, sometimes via Skype – and I manage large projects that involve several freelancers – such as web developers, graphic designers and copy writers – using an online collaborative project management tool called Basecamp (http://basecamphq.com).

There are project management tools included with Elance, for example for signing off milestones, but I prefer to manage projects using the more comprehensive set of tools offered by Basecamp. It can be branded to your business, and I also use this to share files and other deliverables with clients via a 'client login' link on my websites.

Once you have selected your freelancer or team for a project, you can create a new project in Basecamp and assign people logins to it. There are a number of people who I have worked with for years who I regularly assign to projects in this way. You can use it as a messageboard to communicate with your team, share files such as documents, graphics, audio and video, set up to-do lists and assign tasks, list milestones and more. I use Basecamp all the time – to manage client projects, to deliver resources to my workshop participants – I even used it with my publisher to project manage the writing of this book! You can now also use something called Sortfolio (http://sortfolio.com), from the people who brought you Basecamp, to source a web designer.

If you want to collaborate on documents, spreadsheets and presentations in real time with your team or with freelancers, Google Docs (http://docs .google.com) is free and incredibly useful.

However you source, assemble and manage your team, and whether for discrete projects or ongoing business functions, there are online tools to help you find help with your online marketing. But don't let go of everything. Remember that the reason your online marketing works, particularly your social media marketing, is YOU. Your

❝ the reason your online marketing works is YOU ❞ authentic voice, personality and passion. That's probably part of the reason you started your own business in the first place: to do things in your own unique way, follow your own interests and pursue a passion. Never be afraid to be yourself online. You may be surprised how much business this generates – even unintentionally. Resist the urge to be a bland corporate clone, or to hand your social media presence over to someone else. You can't outsource you.

Outsource the parts of your marketing, and your business, that you either can't do, don't want to do, or don't have the time to do. Then focus on what you enjoy, what you do best, and where you can add the greatest value to your business. And have fun with it: you've worked hard to build your business – now see it grow with online marketing!

Take action

- **Audit** your tasks and decide what help you need.

- **Find** help via Elance.

- **Manage** your projects with Basecamp.

- **Do what you do best** – and outsource the rest!

An A–Z of online marketing

Aggregation – the process of gathering together content from websites, blogs, or other forms of social media, often using RSS feeds. Content may be aggregated in a newsreader, website, personalised home page, or even Facebook profiles, groups or pages.

Archive – on blogs, archives are collections of older posts usually organised by month. You may still be able to comment on archived items, unless the blogger has closed comments for older items.

Article marketing – sites such as Ezine (www.ezine.com) enable you to write articles for distribution to a wide audience, with your biography, byline and a link to your business. Well-written articles increase your credibility and attract new leads, but they can also boost your search engine rankings due to incoming links from these high-ranking sites.

Authenticity – the sense that something or someone is 'real'. Blogs, podcasts, Twitter updates, etc. enable people to publish content and engage in conversations that help them develop an authentic voice online. If you can show personality, passion, and the person behind your business, you will build more trust than a bland corporate voice.

Avatar – a graphical image representing people online. Your avatar is your 'character' in virtual worlds such as Second Life. You can build your avatar with the body, clothes, behaviours, gender and name of your choice. This may or may not be an authentic representation of the person behind the keyboard.

Blog – a website with dated items of content (or 'posts') in reverse chronological order. Posts are usually organised into categories, may also be tagged with keywords, and should allow comments. Blog posts can include images, video and audio as well as text. Blogs can usually be subscribed to using an RSS feed and are great for driving traffic to a site and boosting search engine rankings. Blogs are easy to set up using tools such as Blogger, Typepad and WordPress.

Blogosphere – the term used to describe the totality of blogs on the Internet, and the conversations taking place within that online space.

Blogroll – a list of favourite blogs displayed in the sidebar of a blog, showing who the blogger reads regularly.

Call to action – a clear message contained on a website or piece of social media such as a blog post, podcast or video, to encourage people to do something specific as a result of engaging with your online media. Once you've got someone on to your website, or to listen to your podcast, etc., what do you want them to do? Sign up to your newsletter, download a white paper, visit your blog?

Categories – pre-specified ways to organise content, or a taxonomy – for example a list of categories in the sidebar of a blog that allows you to browse a blog by subject.

Comments – blogs may allow readers to add comments under posts, and may also provide a feed for comments as well as for posts. That means you can keep up with conversations without having to revisit the site to check whether anything has been added.

Online **communities** are groups of people communicating mainly through the Internet. They may be members of a community website, or members of a group on a generic social network (such as a Facebook group). Blog-based communities also exist as communities of people who are regular readers of a blog. These groups may be reached via an email list where they have registered to receive updates by email, or via a Facebook message or a tweet, depending on which tool is used.

Content may refer to text, images, video, audio, or any other material that is on the Internet.

Content management system (CMS) – a piece of software that allows you to add to, edit and update content on your site with no need for technical knowledge of HTML code. WordPress can be used as a CMS.

Conversation through blogging, commenting or contributing to forums is the currency of social networking.

Conversational index – a measure of the impact of a blog, calculated as the number of comments divided by the number of posts, either for a whole blog, a blog category or a time period. Aim for a number greater than 1.

Creative Commons (http://creativecommons.org) – an alternative to copyright that facilitates the sharing of content online by attaching a Creative Commons licence specifying, for example, that content may be reused with attribution.

Cross-browser compatibility – test your website to make sure it works in all major browsers, including Internet Explorer, Firefox, Safari, Google Chrome and Opera.

Crowdsourcing refers to harnessing the skills and enthusiasm of those outside your business who are prepared to volunteer their time contributing content and solving problems.

Culture – social media only works well in a culture of openness, authenticity, trust and two-way communication. It is a commitment rather than a tactic, and culture and attitude are as important as tools. It can be hard for large corporations to use social media because it is a personal medium where authenticity matters. It's often easier for small businesses and individuals.

Dashboard – the 'back-end' control centre of (e.g.) your blog, from where you can manage posts, comments, pages, blogroll, categories, plugins and your blog's appearance via themes and widgets. Can also refer to your dashboard on your web stats or email marketing service etc.

Events – on Facebook, events can be created by individuals, groups or pages. You can also organise events in LinkedIn and other social networks. Great for promoting launches, seminars and other events where you have a following on these networks.

Feed – see RSS feed.

Forums are discussion areas on websites, where people can post messages or comment on existing messages. Before blogs developed, email lists and forums were the main means of conversing online. Forums are useful where you want an open-ended discussion on a specific topic on your website over a longer period of time than a blog post would normally facilitate. Examples of this might include support forums where users of your product share knowledge and advice. These are commonly used by software businesses. Forum discussions are often a feature available on social networking sites, such as on Facebook pages or Flickr groups.

Friends, on social networking sites such as Facebook and MySpace, are contacts whose profile you link to in your profile. On some sites people have to accept your friend request before you are connected. On Twitter they are called followers and on LinkedIn they are called contacts.

Groups – in the social networking sense, groups are pages that can be set up by anyone with a profile and invite others to join. They usually give members the ability to contribute content, such as posting links, images and videos or writing on the wall of a Facebook group, contributing images to a Flickr group, and engaging in forum discussions. Groups are useful for encouraging interaction between members.

Hashtags – are used in Twitter to group tweets (updates) together by subject. They are included in a tweet, as e.g. #swineflu to track topical subjects, and often used at conferences where people are tweeting from presentations, such as #media140. Some conferences will pre-announce the hashtag to be used. Otherwise the most popular one emerges. You don't need to register them anywhere – just make them up. Hashtags become links that can be clicked on to view a timeline of everyone's tweets including that hashtag.

Information architecture is a term used to describe the way content is organised on a website, usually displayed as a flowchart of key pages.

Lurkers are people who read but don't contribute or add comments to forums or blogs. The 1 per cent rule of thumb suggests that about 1 per cent of people contribute new content to an online community, another 9 per cent comment, and the rest lurk. However, they are not necessarily passive, since content consumed may lead to interaction elsewhere, especially if you are clear about your call to action.

Measurement – social media metrics is an emerging discipline. It is possible to track the impact of your social media use with a combination of web-stats packages (such as Google Analytics or Clicky Web Analytics), number tracking (group members, fans, followers, subscriptions, downloads or views), calls to action, surveys, and unique landing pages/click-throughs. For blogs, an important measure is your Conversational Index.

Microblogging – sites such as Twitter that allow personal updates of up to 140 characters. By using separate web tools such as Twitterfeed, they can also be used to promote blogs and other RSS feeds by generating an automatic update to 'followers' whenever new content is published. Through widgets, Twitter updates can also be pulled into websites. Other microblogging sites include Plurk and Jaiku.

Newsreader – a website or desktop tool that acts as an aggregator, gathering content from blogs and similar sites using RSS feeds so you can read the content in one place, instead of having to visit different sites.

Pay per click (PPC) – any form of online advertising where you pay a small amount each time someone clicks on your ad, including Google AdWords and Facebook Social Ads.

Pages – on Facebook, pages provide much of the same functionality as groups, plus some extra functions such as adding many of the same applications you can add to your profile. This can be useful for pulling in a blog via RSS, adding an app that enables user reviews, etc.

Participation – or participatory culture is used to describe a way of doing things in which people use social media to share and collaborate in a way that encourage openness and transparency.

Permalink – the address (URL) of a specific blog post – its 'permanent link'. The blog post title usually links to the permalink.

a personalised home page is essentially an aggregator. It is a service offered by sites including Google (www.google.com/ig), Pageflakes (www.pageflakes.com) and Netvibes (www.netvibes.com). They allow you to pull in content from a range of websites using RSS feeds, including blogs.

Photo sharing – uploading, organising and sharing your digital images to a website like Flickr.

Pingback – lets you know if someone links to one of your blog posts and automatically notifies you, so you can see what people are writing about you.

Podcast – audio or video files than can be subscribed to using RSS and automatically downloaded whenever a new show is published. You don't need an iPod to listen to a podcast – about 50 per cent of people who subscribe to podcasts listen (or watch) online.

A **post** is an item of content on a blog. Usually text, but can also be images, video or audio.

Profiles – the information that you provide about yourself when signing up for a social networking site. As well as a picture and basic information, this may include your personal and business interests, a 'blurb' about yourself, and tags to help people search for like-minded people.

Retweet – a retweet is a Twitter status update that is quoted or passed on. Either use the synatx: 'RT @getuptospeed:', followed by the text you are quoting; or click the Retweet link which becomes visible when you hover over a tweet.

RSS – short for 'Really Simple Syndication'. This allows you to subscribe to content on blogs and other social media and have it delivered to you through a feed. Blogs you subscribe to may be displayed in an aggregator website like Google Reader directly on your desktop using software called a newsreader. Podcasts are usually managed through a service such as iTunes.

Search – people search for information on the Internet using a search engine, of which Google is the most widely used. But they also search Facebook, Twitter, YouTube, iTunes, etc., so it it important to have a presence on these sites too. People also search for blogs on specialist search engines such as Technorati (www.technorati.com) or Google Blogsearch (http://blogsearch.google.com).

Search engine marketing (SEM) – a form of online marketing that promotes websites by increasing their visibility in search engines such as Google, Yahoo or Bing. People rarely click beyond the first two or three pages of results, so it is important to improve your position on these sites. This is done through a combination of search engine optimisation (SEO) and paying for placement in search engine results pages (SERPs), for example using Google AdWords.

Search engine optimisation (SEO) – the process of improving the volume or quality of traffic to a website from 'natural' search results as opposed to paid-for placements on SERPs. This involves editing the content and HTML code of a website to increase its relevance to specific keywords and to remove barriers to the indexing activities of search engines.

SERP – Search engine results page.

Social bookmarking – saving the address of a website or item of content on a social bookmarking site like Delicious. If you add tags, others can search your bookmarks too.

Social currency – you need to use social media to be able to use it for marketing purposes. By being present in the social media space (e.g. having a Facebook profile, a blog, a Twitter account), you build 'social currency'. This gives you 'permission' to use the medium to communicate your marketing message – so long as it is relevant and useful to the people you are communicating with. You can't just spam a Facebook group!

Social media may be thought of as the collection of tools people use to publish, converse and share content online, including blogs, podcasts, video and social networks. Social media marketing is an approach to marketing based on building relationships with people online. It may be thought of as permission-based marketing or conversational marketing.

Social networking sites are places where users can create a profile for themselves, and socialise with their network of friends and contacts using a range of tools such as adding friends, posting messages, links and other content, importing blogs, and creating groups, pages and events. The most popular include Facebook, MySpace and LinkedIn. Twitter may also be thought of as a social network.

Subscribing – the online equivalent of signing up for a magazine: you get new content delivered as it is published. Relates to blogs via RSS feeds, but also podcasts (via e.g. iTunes), YouTube channels, Twitter feeds, email lists, etc.

Tags – keywords attached to a blog post, bookmark, photo or other item of content so you and others can find them easily through searches and aggregation. Tags can usually be freely chosen – and so form part of a *folksonomy* – while categories are predetermined and are part of a *taxonomy*.

Tag cloud – a widget you can add to your blog to show the most commonly used tags. The more often a tag is used, the larger the font size. Your readers can see at a glance what you write about, and click on the tags displayed, making it another way to navigate to your blog's content.

Trackbacks – provided by some blogs as a facility for other bloggers to leave an automatic comment. They are usually indicated as a specific URL, often the permalink for a particular blog post. By using this URL as the link for someone else's blog post that you link to on your own blog, an extract of your linking text automatically appears as a comment on the original blog post.

URL – stands for 'unique resource locator', and is the technical term for a web address e.g. http://www.getuptospeed.biz.

Unique URL or **unique landing page** – a web address that is only ever mentioned in one place, such as a podcast, video or another website (including e.g. Flickr or Twitter). The URL then automatically refers on to the page you want people to land on such as the ordering page for a book, a sign-up page for an email newsletter, etc. This enables you to track exactly how many people who took action landed on your ordering page as a result of watching a video, listening to a podcast or visiting a website.

Usability testing – you should test how easy it is to use your site with a variety of experienced and non-experienced users within your target market. Do this by observing them complete a specific task – such as using a contact form or locating a specific product or piece of content – and take notes. Make changes to your site if testing throws up issues that need addressing.

User-generated content (UGC) – any text, photos or other content that is contributed to a site by its users. Examples are Wikipedia, Digg and Flickr.

Video has taken off since the wide uptake of broadband. Sites such as YouTube, Vimeo and blip.tv make it easy to upload and share videos. These sites also provide code for each video to enable you to embed the video in a blog post or website. It's usually best to keep them short – no more than 3 minutes, provide useful content that people will value, and provide a URL for people to click through to.

Virtual worlds – online places like Second Life (http://secondlife.com) where you can create a representation of yourself (an avatar) and socialise with other residents. In some ways these are just another social network – it is usually possible to join groups and add people to your friends list – but one with a rich graphical interface that has to be learned first, creating a higher barrier to entry than, say, Facebook.

Web 2.0 – a term coined by O'Reilly Media in 2004 to describe a second generation of web services including blogs, wikis, social networking sites and other Internet-based services that emphasise collaboration, sharing, participation and self-publishing rather than less interactive, static websites (Web 1.0). What we used to call Web 2.0 a few years ago is now more commonly referred to as social media.

White paper – a free downloadable document, usually a report or guide, used to educate people and help them make decisions. Often used to generate sales leads, establish thought leadership, make a business case, or to educate customers. Can be used as an incentive to sign up to your email list.

Widgets are stand-alone mini-applications you can embed in websites or a desktop. These may help you to do things like subscribe to a feed, pull in content from another site, display comments from your Twitter followers, etc.

Wiki – a web page or website that can be edited collaboratively. The best known example is Wikipedia (http://wikipedia.org), an encyclopaedia created by thousands of contributors across the world. Depending on their permissions level, people can add and/or edit pages. Create your own wiki using www.wikispaces.com.

Wireframe – a simple diagram showing the layout of key elements of a web page.

Wisdom of crowds – the idea that individual contributions to a website – such as items of content, rankings and ratings – produce robust, reliable results that are greater than the sum of their parts. For example, Wikipedia is more reliable and authoritative than often thought, since inaccurate or insufficiently referenced information will soon be challenged or edited by others. Digg is another example.

Index